GRACE
IN
CHAOS

LEAH SCOTT

 FriesenPress

Suite 300 - 990 Fort St
Victoria, BC, V8V 3K2
Canada

www.friesenpress.com

ISBN
978-1-5255-7669-0 (Hardcover)
978-1-5255-7670-6 (Paperback)
978-1-5255-7671-3 (eBook)

1. FAMILY & RELATIONSHIPS, PARENTING, MOTHERHOOD

Distributed to the trade by The Ingram Book Company

Dedicated to Jack, Luke, and Brielle. It is because of you I am on this ride of my life and there is no greater joy in my life than being your mom. From the moment I held each of you in my arms I was forever changed.

Table of Contents

Introduction

To the mom that is holding her newborn that has not stopped crying for hours and you feel desperate and alone, I see you.

To the mom that has not slept through the night in years, I see you.

To the mom in tears, locked in the bathroom because she feels overwhelmed by the constant input by toddlers and all their needs and she needs a few moments of peace, I see you.

To the mom of the toddler that is melting down after getting exactly what he asked for on the color of plate he asked for, but it is not right and he won't tell you why and you can't read his mind, I see you.

To the mom wondering if she should just make a bed in the back of the vehicle because she spends so much time in there running kids around that she might as well move in, I see you.

To the mom who feels like she has lost who she was and, while being a mom is the best thing that has happened to her, she also feels guilty for missing having another purpose, I see you.

To the mom of a child with special needs who feels exhausted because the advocacy for her child never ends, and neither does the judgment, I see you.

To the mom of teens who is weary from the emotional toll of the battle that comes with them testing their boundaries, yet still needing you, but never being able to say it in a nice way, I see you.

To the mom that stays home with her kids and wants some time away from them, I see you.

To the mom that works out of the home and wishes she was home more often and is weary from the juggling, I see you.

To the mom that runs the house while her partner works away, I see you.

To the single mom that is doing it all, I see you.

I see you. I think you are amazing, remarkable human beings and I want this book to bless you deeply. I want you know that you are not alone in this journey and I am cheering you on so hard.

Motherhood is hard. There is no denying it. We are hard on ourselves and often also hard on each other. I cannot count how many times I have told myself that I am a bad mom or I am failing when we have a rough day, or a tough incident in our home. What if we gave ourselves grace? Full-blown grace. To ourselves. In the Bible, grace is defined as God's unmerited favor. His love, blessing, and favour despite our lack of deserving it. So, what if we loved ourselves and reminded ourselves that we are always doing our best, even when it is hard and we don't feel like we deserve it? I also found this definition of grace in the Cambridge Dictionary: "the charming quality of being polite and pleasant, or a willingness to be fair and to forgive." What if we held onto this quality for ourselves? And other moms? We are so hard on ourselves, and we are also hard on other moms. Even if we don't say something to them, we often judge when someone does something different than us. But what if we had the charming qualities of being polite and pleasant, and were willing to be fair to ourselves and others, and forgive both ourselves and others freely and willingly? Imagine if we operated from this place of value on ourselves as moms? One of my deepest desires is for moms to know their worth, to see themselves as the remarkable women they are, to give themselves so much grace and to be the champion for other moms. We are all in this together.

Seven years ago, I became a mom. I had no idea what I was getting into, but I sure didn't think it was going to be that hard. I felt pretty confident in how relatively easy this was going to be. It did not take me long to realize how wrong I was. I became passionate about talking to other moms about our experiences, because I felt like there was so much that was never talked about. Many times, I felt like I was going crazy, or felt totally alone and said something to another mom, and she would say, "Oh yeah, that happened to me too," or, "Oh yeah, that's just a thing." I remember wondering why no one told me 'That was a thing,' and saved me from many of those feelings.

My heart's desire over these last seven years has been to come alongside other parents, because dads are incredible too and experience some of this as well, but especially moms. To look at each other in the day-to-day trenches and even just make a comment to a total stranger to let her know, 'I have been here too and felt all these emotions.' The highs of holding your baby for the first time or watching their milestones, and the lows of missing some of those milestones. Hearing them say, "I love you mommy" as they squeeze your cheeks and you feel like your heart will explode out of your chest, but then how that same heart feels shattered when they look at you in anger and tell you that they hate you or you aren't the best mommy. Those moments in a public place where someone tells you how beautiful and well behaved your children are and you beam and say thank you, only to have your children follow it up with a full-blown meltdown in a store where you end up carrying out a screaming child, and you swear you passed about ten judging glances on your way out. Parenting feels like one giant oxymoron most of the time. You want to hold on to all the good of each stage and yet you want to rush yourself out of it at the same time, because every stage and season has its own challenges.

I love to observe moms. Through social media, in life, out and about wherever I am. Even my friends. Everyone has their strengths and weaknesses. Sometimes there are those moms that you see and you feel a pang of resentment, or maybe jealousy, that they seem to have it all together in a season where you felt, or feel, like one hot mess. I assure you, even that mom does not have it all together, all the time, either. I had people ask me in a season where I literally felt like the wheels were falling off at any given moment, how I managed to do it. I would literally laugh out loud because what, to them, looked like me doing it all, to me, felt like one giant disaster most days and certainly did not feel like a season of put-together-ness or accomplishing much of anything. Those same moms that I have had the opportunity to observe, and wonder how they do it, I have also had the opportunity to bless them with a hot drink on a hard day. I have seen them in some of those moments where they do not have it all pulled together. I enjoy blessing them, and I file it away that nothing is as it seems in a small window of time, at a glance, or on social media. We all thrive sometimes, survive sometimes, win some days, and feel like we failed others. At the core of who we are as mothers, we experience much of the same feelings, emotions, challenges, wins and losses. We are all human and deeply striving for what is best for our families.

Another observation of mine is that we all have stages in our children's lives that we love and others that we struggle with. For some, the baby stage, that newborn phase of life, is their jam. They savour it, love it, and while it is still hard, something about it fuels them. For others, those first three months are the absolute hardest three months of their life. Some of it may depend a little bit on how that baby made an appearance earthside, which can certainly have an impact on it all, depending on how much recovery is involved for mom. But in general, I have learned that we need to both make space for those that do not like a season or stage and struggle through it, and for those that do love a particular season or stage more than we did. It can be easy to both resent someone that loves something that you did not, and to judge the person that does not love something that you did. Just as there are infinite ways to love and care for your children and each of them will require different things from you, there are equally as many ways to embrace and support the differences between us as mothers and what we love, what we struggle with and how we could all use a little boost of grace in the chaos of motherhood.

The message I want to settle deep inside your heart is that you are not alone in this journey. The feelings that you feel, so many moms before you have felt too. The dark days and the moments where you sit on the floor and cry with your babies because you just cannot even do one more thing, I have too. When you feel crazy like you want to pull them in and push them away, keep them small and make them big, where you want to cry but you have to laugh to survive, where you want bedtime to feel precious but it actually feels like a hostage negotiation, that there are thousands of other moms feeling the same way. Let us bring this into the light.

Other people's lives are not just Instagram highlight reels, while you can't even leave the house without food on your shirt and you haven't showered in who knows how many days. It is not wrong to highlight the good. Practising gratitude and sharing joy is essential to surviving motherhood and we need to celebrate every little incredible moment, even if it is that no one fought in the last three minutes. However, we also need to be real with each other. Judge less, listen more. Be aware of what our friends may not be saying behind the scenes. Reach out to each other. Bring your friend a tea. If you know she has a favourite kind but you don't drink tea, still add it to your grocery list because it will bless her that you have it at your house if she comes over. If you pick up a Starbucks drink in the drive through because your day sucked, grab one for your friend and drop it off on your way home. I guarantee, the joy of blessing your friend will bless you and give you a moment of joy in a terrible day.

Let us love each other harder. Let us come together as a collective whole of hot messes and carry each others' burdens. Maybe your babies are now little kids. Even if you don't have baby fever, hold that baby that wants to be held every single second and give that mom a few minutes of freedom. When a mom of teens tells you, in the trenches of toddlerhood, to "Enjoy it now, just wait until they are teens," don't resent her for forgetting what it is like to have the constant input of toddlers, but look at it as a way to maybe rally around her. Teen issues can cause a lot of grief to those mom hearts, and maybe she is the one that needs a hot drink or a little note of encouragement from a friend.

We have morphed into a society that seems to pride itself on being busy. Our schedules are often maxed out and we are on the move from the minute our feet hit the floor until we call it a wrap on another day. It can become so difficult to even look up and notice what is happening around us. In this, I believe we have lost the opportunity to really connect with people, to sit and share meals together with another family, to come alongside each other in comradery and friendship. Especially once our babies are bigger and the activities are keeping us on the move all the time. But we were created for relationship and companionship. Not just in our marriages and relationships, but in our friendships too. When was the last time you got together with a group of moms? Where you did not feel guilty taking a night out to connect with your people? How do we keep our finger on the pulse of our mom friends if we never take the time to connect with them? We must come alongside each other and bear these burdens, because no one gets it like we do.

I recently read a story on the internet about a community of women that used to gather at the river to wash clothes together. When they got washing machines, there was a rise in the depression level of these women. Why? Because they no longer had a place to meet, to talk, to share, to connect. The lack of connection, the lack of needing each other does not serve us. There is a reason the phrase "It takes a village to raise a child" was created. We still say it, we still hear it, but do we believe it?

My life is full. We have activities and commitments, but we love to help other people when they need help. We have interests, and hobbies that we like to do. But what fills my soul the most? When I connect with others. When I sit with other moms and I don't apologize for my messy house, but I welcome them in. This is hard for me. I love a clean, tidy house. I love to look like I have it all together. But in order to have all of that, I might miss out of the blessing that it is to love another mom. To make extra dinner and deliver it to someone else. To just sit and be present with each other and truly deep dive into how amazing and hard motherhood is; to learn from each other and find new ideas to try, while your kids run wild and scream and make a giant mess.

This past weekend, I washed my floor for the first time in four months. Yes, four months since I washed my floor. My sweet husband assures me he washed it some time in there, so bless him. I said to two of my best friends, looks like I can run a home business, write a book, invest in the lives of others, be a mom and a wife, but the cost is a clean floor. One day I will have a clean floor again. But in the meantime, I am going to commit to spending more of my time coming alongside my friends. Getting into the trenches that are messy. Talking about the good and the bad. It is in these moments where we feel heard and validated that I think we can truly set ourselves free as moms. Together we can accept the hard and the ugly, but also laugh about it, cry about it, and find the perspective to be grateful for the hard, so that the amazing just seems that much better. Just being heard and understood can be the one thing a mom needs to let her know that she is not alone, not failing, not a terrible mom for those emotions and thoughts that are running through her head; instead, she is normal and it is actually going to be okay.

1.

Moving from the Dream of Motherhood to the Reality

Motherhood. For many of us this is something long dreamed of, for others, it's something they are determined to steer clear of. Some people in the middle feel undecided as to whether or not they want to embark on the journey of motherhood. However, typically speaking, women have this need to nurture. It is beautiful and remarkable. I see this in my daughter, that there is something different from her brothers, and it's not because of gender roles, upbringing, or being directed in any certain direction. It's just there. It is in the fabric of who she is. She loves to be a momma to her babies. I literally find dolls, stuffed animals and Barbies tucked in all over my house with dish towels, regular towels, blankets, pillow cases, whatever she can find. My house is often a hotbed of babies napping in all the random spaces, including the centre of my kitchen floor, not to be woken up unless deemed appropriate by their doting and attentive momma.

I was one of the former girls. From a young age, I wanted to babysit kids. I was over the moon every time a cousin was added to our family. One time, when I was about twelve, I got to have my toddler cousin stay at our house and I was his primary caregiver while my aunt and uncle were away. In hindsight, I probably didn't do it all, as imagined in the depths of my memory; my own mom was probably very present in the overall care of that toddler. But his crib was in my room, and I was his person for that time that he was there.

I wanted to have six kids and my main dream in life was to be a mom. I'm sure if you asked my older brother, he would be quick to tell you that I did my best to mother him through our childhood, much to his annoyance I'm sure. I took my role very seriously to be the nurturer, the finder of all the things, and the keeper of every detail that people in the house needed to know. I baked, cleaned, and took great pride in all of it. In my mind, all of this was preparing to make some man to the luckiest guy in the world to have me for a wife, and those six kids to be the luckiest kids in the world to have me as their mom.

Fast forward to my twenties where I was going to do all my planned education, and by then I would be with the man of my dreams and we would get married and spend a couple of years together, and travel. This would be followed by three or four babies, my having decided that six was way out of my league, having a little further insight as an adult. However, unbeknownst to me, before all of this was going to come together for me, there was going to be an extended season of learning to be content on my own. I remember at times, while actually thoroughly enjoying my singlehood, crying some tears that, *what if* motherhood wasn't going to happen for me? How was that even possible? Wasn't this my dream? Wasn't this what I had prepared for my entire life, while cleaning, baking, and dreaming of the days when all of this hard work was going to make me the most amazing mom on earth? Where I would bake for my kids, make them fun birthday cakes, and throw them the best parties? I was going to love to do crafts, read stories, and lay with the kids at night for hours. I was going to rub backs, stroke foreheads, whisper all the words of affirmation that they would ever need, and literally be mother of the year, for their whole lives.

The year I turned thirty, I started dating the man that I would share my life with. About three years later, we were ready for kids. I had been preparing my whole life for this; I thought I was pretty great with other people's babies so this was going to be so easy. I mean really, how hard could it be, right?

We got pregnant with our first baby and I had a horrible pregnancy, with unbearable sciatic pain and nausea and vomiting from start to finish. There was no glowing, happy, dreamy pregnant life around here. Growing a human is no joke. I think that growing a human is the hardest thing on earth. For real. While it would seem to the unknowing, unaware person, that you just go about life and a human grows in there; what's the big deal? Then you get pregnant and within about four or five weeks, give or take, you start to feel weird. The period cramps that were supposed to be gone for at least the next nine months now come all day, every day, because there is something strange happening in there. Things are stretching, moving, getting more relaxed and, while the baby is literally like the size of a pencil eraser or less, all the hormones are wreaking havoc on your body. Then the nausea starts to settle in. It's like you have that foreboding nausea that you typically get before the stomach flu, but it *never ends*. Maybe you are one of the ones that vomited all the time; maybe you just felt horrible. Regardless of how you felt, you are now faced with the fact that you have the pressure of taking care of this little life inside of you, and making all the right decisions to keep it healthy, safe, well nourished, and cared for in your womb for the next nine months—but all you can do is vomit up anything healthy you go

3

near. All you crave-is Pepsi and greasy cheeseburgers and french fries, or candies, chips, and slushies, or pickles, or whatever your vice is, but it *very rarely* seems to be that you crave vegetables or anything good and healthy for your babe that you can even begin to consider holding down. This starts the spiral of mom guilt. You are about five weeks into this journey of motherhood, your child isn't even on the outside yet—heck it hasn't even started registering as the size of any type of fruit on the fruit scale that you get weekly updates on your app about—and you are facing mom guilt. Welcome to the party, mommas. You're officially part of the club.

Now you are showing, and people are starting to ask you all the questions. "Are you finding out what you are having?" Followed by, "Oh, I don't know how you can handle not knowing!!" Or, "Oh, I never wanted to know, it's the only good surprise left in life!!" Or, "Are you having a hospital birth? A home birth? A water birth? A C-section?" "Are you using a midwife or a doctor?" And on it goes. Then the horror stories start about how awful people's pregnancies were and how awful their labor and deliveries were. They want to talk about how terrible it was to have a baby in the fall and be pregnant all summer, or what month is the best to have a baby, when clearly at this point you have no control over seasons, months, or when this baby is going to make an appearance. Bless them all. It is overwhelming at times. Some people are downright offensive and others are a gift. The reality here, is that you are growing a human. You are amazing.

Now it comes the time for this baby to join you earthside. Many women, especially first-time moms, have a birth plan. However, often how babies arrive may not have happened the way their mothers imagined it would. There is a high likelihood that your birth plan didn't go off without a hitch. The opinion of others is irrelevant. Are you happy with your choice? Is this what you have dreamed of? Yes? Mission accomplished. If that birth plan didn't happen, maybe you ended up with the C-section you were dead set against, or you now have a traumatic birth story that you may or may not share with future pregnant moms. Please, please, *please* remember that this does not define you as a mom. This does *not* change the amazing human you are for bringing this life into the world. That *you* are remarkable. *You* are the most amazing mom for that baby. This is your story, and it might not matter to you that the plan changed. For others, a traumatic birth can be devastating. If that is you, please make sure you find someone to talk to about those feelings, because you need to figure out where to put that grief that it didn't go as planned, so that you can savour the fact that your babe is here. If I had to choose the single greatest high on the planet, it would be that moment when I held my baby for the first time. Whether it's your first or your sixth, *that* moment is the best feeling on earth. May that moment be the balm to your soul over whatever else went on before. I don't completely buy into the "You forget everything once the baby is out" theory, but I do think that moment does hold so much magic that it does allow you to consider that you would, in fact, do this again. Maybe even more than once.

2.

Baby Bliss... or Is It???

This is the moment you have been dreaming of, quite possibly for almost your entire life. It seems like there are a lot of girls out there that are babies, and then at about eighteen months old, they become mommies. Obviously, just in their minds, but they identify all babies and toddlers as babies that they can love and nurture. They gravitate toward them, and want to help them in every way.

My daughter has access to all the same toys as her two older brothers. She's as rough-and-tumble as they come. She had two older brothers with lots of action figures. My daughter can swaddle and rock Spiderman and Ironman with the best of them. As I mentioned earlier, she loves to nurture babies and she gravitates toward dolls. Loving and caring for them. She cradles them in her arms and whispers, "It's okay baby, Mommy's here," into their hair. It's inherent in her to "mother" her dolls, her brothers, her stuffed animals, and every other baby and toddler she comes into contact with.

So here you are, with your very own baby. Maybe you've dreamed of this your whole life, and maybe you didn't want kids, but under some circumstances it happened anyway. Regardless, you are cradling this little human being that you have grown, loved, and dreamed of for the last nine-ish months of your life. Is this the moment you dreamed it would be? Is everything perfect? I think the large majority of mothers would say, yes this moment is, in fact, *more* than they ever imagined, especially if it is their first baby. If it isn't your first, then you knew what was coming—but every delivery and experience has its own highs and lows. However, for some mothers there is so much going on in that moment that it feels like you were robbed of the dream that you were expecting. I want to talk to you first.

Maybe you didn't come through the delivery healthy, and are in need of medical intervention and can't hold your baby, or your baby is in distress, or has been born with an anomaly you were not expecting. Maybe you aren't bonding for some reason, or there is trauma that happened to you to conceive this child, or trauma in your past that is putting up walls. There is so much that can be complex in this very moment of having your baby that can change how you respond and react to this new child. You may feel like everyone is expecting you to fall deeply and madly in love with this baby, but in that moment you are not feeling all the things you expected to, or you feel others expect you to. It may feel traumatic and devastating. Right then and there, you feel like you have already failed this baby. Sweet mommas, I hope that by the time you are reading this, someone has already told you that you *did not fail!* Life is hard and unexpected, and that very moment that you were in bears so much emotion, hormones, and complexity that it is impossible to even begin to navigate it at all. And if the road to this moment was treacherous for you, and you barely made it to this point, you may just have been hanging on for dear life for your own survival. Maybe literally or even just figuratively. But either way, sometimes, we need to embrace survival for ourselves *before* we can ever get to the place where we can offer safety, survival and unreserved love for another human being.

People are hard and there can be judgment. Both from yourself and from others, and you might be living under the weight of this guilt and shame of not being the mother you felt like you were supposed to be in that moment. If no one has told you before now, you are not bound to this guilt and shame. This does not define you as a mother and it does not write your story. I am so sorry that this is how you and you child got your start together. My heart actually hurts as I write this thinking about this very experience that some mothers go through. We only get one shot at bringing each baby into the world and when you don't get a re-do, it can be so difficult to accept that reality, move past it, and find healing. But I'm here to tell you that even if you have this experience as part of your story, you are still the mom that God chose for your baby. You are still the one that God gave this good gift to, to raise that child the way it needs to be raised. You are enough. You are worthy. If you are struggling under the weight of this, you need to reach out to someone to help you process that part of your story and place it where it needs to be so that you can find the freedom to embrace the gift that you are to your child.

Now, for the majority of moms. Your baby has been placed into your arms. You've dreamed of this moment for, at the very least, nine months, but likely longer. It really is better than you could have ever imagined. You literally lose yourself in this moment. Maybe there are tears, and maybe there are not. Regardless, this moment is burned into the fabric of your being and you get totally lost in it. As I mentioned earlier, there is something so magical about this moment that it, quite possibly, is what will carry you for the next three months, if not twenty years.

There will be moments where you stare at this little human in your arms in utter and complete love and amazement that they are *yours*. You don't have to give them back (as opposed to the moments where you don't *get* to give them back) and you get to leave the hospital with this little human being. You may or may not even look around quickly for a brief moment as you leave the hospital to see if it's really true, no one is going to say you can't go! But enter in reality. It can start so quickly after the initial high of delivery.

Now it's time to breastfeed this baby. It's supposed to be easy, right? God created us to breastfeed, how hard can that be? Put that baby to the breast to latch and let them be nourished. But wait! You have to get them to latch. When I think of the word latch, I think of something closed tightly. Which, if a part of my body is in the way of that latch, it is going to hurt. Well, that's not really much different than a latching baby. All lactation consultants will tell you that latching is not supposed to hurt. Which is true. Yet, I doubt there is any mom that has not experienced the knife-like pain of sore, painful, cracked nipples because that latch is never 100 percent perfect all the time. Yowza! That is a feeling that you will never forget. It will cause you to put up "Do Not Cross" tape across your chest for the sake of your partner for the foreseeable future, and will cause you to cry tears along with your screaming baby while considering, at least once, if perhaps this is a terrible idea and formula is the way to go.

Breastfeeding at the beginning is hard for many women. You long for it to be easy as you gaze down at your baby, but typically it takes time for the milk to come in; and that in-between period means you are basically a 24-hour diner. You are exhausted because you probably haven't sleep well for weeks, especially the last day or two; hormones plummet, and changes are coming fast and furious. If this your first baby, no one ever explained to you how you feel like a sour, soggy milk cow. Your body hurts, nothing feels right, people have been looking at all your most private parts for days now, your boobs are constantly out, and every person you know wants to just pop in and say hello. Due to all the visitors that mean so well and want to hold the baby, you are only getting your baby when they are frantic to eat because you dared take them off the breast to allow someone to hold them. This requires you to completely expose yourself to get them to latch on and somewhere along the line, some well-meaning friend or family will assure you that they don't mind if you just go ahead and feed that baby while they are there, but in your mind you are scream-ing, "But I don't want you to see my breasts, please get out!!"

With my third baby, she ended up in the intensive care nursery for the first five days of her life. Her breathing was an issue and she needed some support. So there I was, after three babies in three and a half years, thinking 'I am a new mom and breast feeding veteran, sitting in a hospital room away from my baby, feeling all the emotions, crying my face off, desperately wanting it not to be this way.' The nurse came in and started telling me that I needed to hand-express milk for the first forty-eight hours to get my milk to come in to have some colostrum for my daughter, and to just get that process going. After forty-eight hours I could have a pump. So, she was going to show me how to do this. My husband was in the chair reading his book. He was the picture of support during this entire process, but he wasn't really paying a lot of attention to what was happening.

The nurse started showing me how to essentially milk myself to express milk. After about five minutes of all of this, she casually said, "You know, sometimes husbands step up at this point and they help their wives, and it can be really helpful." I glanced over at my husband who was, at a glance, just sitting in the corner ignoring this entire conversation. I said to the nurse, "At this point I think I'll just leave it as is and do this myself." All I could think in my head was, 'Every single thing about being pregnant and then giving birth and this entire feeling of how my body feels right now, is counterproductive to me *ever* feeling desirable ever again—and having my husband express my milk, like milking a cow, is just icing on the cake.' It was just a hard "no" for me at that point.

After the nurse left, I just said to my husband that I didn't expect him to do it, and he just looked up at me with these kind eyes and said, "I'm so sorry you have to do this. If you need me to I will, but thank you for not asking me to." This is a principle of motherhood: Just because you think you have experience; every child will ensure that they give you new experiences that make you feel like you have never done this before.

Fast forward to day three. When I was a first-time mom, I couldn't believe how many things I just didn't know about or expect. I was a nurse, but it didn't prepare me for giving birth to my own baby. I also did not work in any area that pertained to childbirth and the postpartum period. Day three rolled around and I started to cry. About everything. I'm pretty sure I even said to my husband, "I don't know what's wrong with me and why I can't stop crying." In talking with friends later, they assured me that this was a thing. That on day three (one mom told me it was on day seven for her) you cry all day. I think it has to do with hormone shifts, but goodness, it is a *loonnggg* day. So now I feel like it's my mission in life to make sure that new moms know that if they have a day early on when they cannot stop crying for anything, it's okay. It will pass. You aren't crazy. You aren't a giant failure as a mom like you think you are, and you are going to make it through.

Everyone is different when it comes to their thoughts on having visitors in the hospital and once you get home. I remember going to see so many new moms in the hospital before I had my own babies. Now I look back and cringe at the very thought of how many moms I went to see that I was not really close to, but I felt like it was supportive and kind as a friend or acquaintance to show up see their new baby. Looking back, I'm somewhat horrified by this. No one ever said anything and they were all very gracious about it. They let me hold their sweet sleeping babies and seemed pleased that I stopped by.

I remember talking to a girl that was having her baby soon, and she and her partner had a rule that not even the parents were allowed to come to the hospital to see them. That this was their time with their baby and only theirs to bond. I remember at the time thinking that was so ridiculous and rude to the people around them. That's right, I judged her. Upon having my own babies, I quickly realized why they had set some significant boundaries. I had some serious respect for their willingness to really stake their claim on what *they* wanted as new parents.

With our first baby we had a lot of visitors that popped by, and that was when I realized that it's really hard to always have people coming. You never sleep and are baring your private parts regularly and you and your baby are both still adjusting to each other. Then people want to come. They are so excited for you and they mean well, and you are excited to show off your new baby. However, you are exhausted and want to hold your baby when they don't need to be fed or changed, and just enjoy them. You actually don't want the whole world to see your breasts, even though people have assured you they are fine with it, but you are not. Then, on the off chance that your baby is sleeping, and the nurse hasn't been in to wake you for the hundredth time as you are dozing off, this might be your *only* opportunity for a few minutes of sleep in the foreseeable future and now you are busy making small talk and chatting with the next visitor, who in some of my cases before children, was someone you didn't even know that well and didn't care if they came to visit. My apologies to those friends who wondered why on earth I was making the trek to the hospital when the last time we even saw each other in person was months ago, I truly meant well and thought I was being a lovely person supporting you in this amazing new season of life. Now, I realize that perhaps I was wrong, and a simple card in the mail or text would have been sufficient.

We did love to introduce our family to our new babies: Those were visitors we were thrilled to have. As well as some close friends. And honestly, the people that did come, we were grateful for the gesture (just in case you are reading this now and doing a quick inventory in your head if I am in fact talking to you), but after our first baby, we were a little more honest with people that we would prefer a visit once we were home, and that worked quite well.

All in all, sweet moms that are reading this (and you are either anticipating your first or are still planning on having more children), please feel free to set the boundaries that you want. Maybe you are the person that wants all the friends to come and see you at the hospital rather than when you go home. Enjoy all of those visits!! But if you are not that person, allow me to give you the freedom to say "No, thank you" to visitors, to set boundaries and to ask for what you want as a new mom. This is your time. You only get to savour those sweet early moments while adrenaline is still pumping through your veins for a short time. All the sleep deprivation in the world hasn't set in yet and you are basking in those early hours and days of staring at your little newborn in awe and wonder, thinking about how remarkable this is that they have

13

arrived earthside and you now have the pleasure of soaking them in. If you don't want to share much with others, just say the word. Ask them to come at a later date once you are home and feeling a little more settled.

If you are a friend that has never had babies and you wonder how you can be the most helpful in this season, ask your friend what she actually needs and wants. You are a gift to her. Be gracious. Love her even if you feel like you are a little offended by the boundaries. Know that it is not personal. Also, it would bless her if you showed up at her house later with something practical. Even if you go buy muffins from the store or at the very least, swing by the nearest coffee shop and buy her a drink, show up with something real and practical to meet your friend's physical need. She has not slept in what feels like a million years. She probably hasn't fed herself in hours and she could really use a meal, or some muffins, or fruit and veggies cut up and ready to just grab and eat. Feeding mothers is the single most practical and beneficial thing you can do for your friend in those early days of motherhood.

If you encounter a new mom, consider this: She likely hasn't eaten or slept properly since that little person has arrived. Be a good friend and send her to bed while you either hold the baby or clean the bathroom. You have a lifetime to catch up on her birth story later if she takes you up on the offer. Or, perhaps if she is not willing to go sleep, throw in a load of laundry for her, then grab the stuff in the dryer and fold a load of clothes. Do not sit there and hold her sweet peaceful baby the whole time (unless she insists she needs you to so that she can have a break). For some moms, their baby is not peaceful much and if they are, it would actually bless them to be able to enjoy and bond in that moment rather than to only have that baby while he or she is crying the entire time. Read the situation and ask, in an honest and genuine way, how you can show up to this visit in the most practical and helpful way possible, rather than just to serve your own need for baby snuggles. There will be plenty of those to go around too. But this new mom will most certainly have some needs that have gone unmet, and you could be the one to help her meet at least one of them. I wish I had known better how to care for my friends before I had kids. I had so much more capacity to make a meal, or bake, or grab a hot drink. I just didn't know how valuable that was.

As moms, we fall into this place of feeling like we need to be all the things for everyone, and do all the things for them. I don't know about you, but I feel this weight of guilt settle over me when I allow myself to have help. To be vulnerable. To admit I can't do it all. Like it shows weakness. 'That other mom just had her sixth baby and she's making it look easy, why is my first rocking my world and I haven't been able to feed myself and my husband for weeks now?' 'I haven't showered or left the house since this baby was born and I feel like I'm drowning. That mom over there on baby number four just headed off to the church campout two weeks after having a baby like it was no big deal.' We can spiral so easily into this mindset of needing help, feeling guilty for asking for help, and wondering why we are not able to do it all, when all these moms around us look like they are nailing everything about life and motherhood. I am here to tell you, they probably aren't. But they may just be further along down the path of letting things go, changing the standards, and being forced into the balance that maybe you haven't figured out yet.

This is also a place where we, as new moms, can have a very honest conversation with our partners that we need help. It can be hard to even know which way is up and what your needs are, but the earlier you can start to talk about how overwhelming this feels, and ask for help in practical ways, the easier the transition may be for both of you.

I know I felt this pressure that I put on myself that I was supposed to step into motherhood with grace and ease, and still be the same wife I always was. The reality is, everything was so different now, and I could not still be the exact same person I was before. Every couple is different, and figuring out how to juggle the load will look different. Some husbands get up for all the night time feeds and diaper changes, and then bring baby to mom. My husband slept like the dead, and it was going to be way more work to get him to wake up than it was to just do it myself. However, I think it would have served me well to actually ask him to help me get a nap in more often, or maybe to ask him to take over making dinner after work once in awhile and we could just eat a little later. I could have easily asked him to help me in ways that may have been helpful to me, instead of feeling resentful at times for how hard this felt and that this all fell on me. My husband told me later, that while he was so in love with our children, he didn't feel like he had as much of a role to play when they were so tiny because I had to feed them, and I knew how to hold them and comfort them. He said if he could have gotten all of our kids at eighteen months old when they were more fun to interact with, that he would have been happy. I wanted him to just see that I had needs, and then intuitively meet them—when in reality, he had no idea how to help me. I wish I would have been better at really spelling it out for him and laying aside my pride that I either had to do it all, or that he should just know.

I truly believe that most partners want nothing more than to help and love both their spouse and their baby in that time and we, as moms, could be clearer in what our needs are. It will be different for each of us but I think it could make that time a little easier.

Bear in mind also that this type of communication with your partner will be invaluable for all the years of raising these babies together. Parenthood is never your job and yours alone. So, start the conversation early in how you can lean on your partner as your best ally in this job of raising children.

I call the first baby the "world rocker." This is where everything changes. After this, you are in a groove already of adapting to life with kids. Honestly, in many ways the first can be the hardest as you figure out even how to have to think for more human beings than just yourself. Just like everything, you get better with practise, and parts of it become second nature. Not all of it, but parts of it. If you are in this season of adjusting to your first child, give yourself so much grace as you adjust. You have to figure out for yourself what can give. There is freedom in changing the standards that you held in high regard before you had kids. For some people, doing so will give joy and peace. For others, they do it to survive and accept it as their new reality, but they will always cringe at the thought that their house, for the foreseeable future, will *never* be clean and tidy at the same time. The moment that first little human entered their world, that reality ended. Somehow, even a little human being that takes up about twenty inches of space and can't move themselves, has created this wave of chaos that they will be leaving in their wake, likely for the next twenty years, at least.

For me, it is hard to let go of the fact that I can't be put together all the time and I can't have a clean and tidy house. Because those things still give me joy and they make me feel calmer. I love a tidy space. *But,* when I accept willingly that I have to let that standard go for my mental health, my ability to enjoy my children and watch them be creative it gives me different kind of joy. I work to unapologetically tell people that they are always welcome in my home even if the space might be messy, because I value them and the time spent together. It allows me the gift of choosing relationship over task, which is another place I find joy.

It is always a work in progress not to compare myself to others. To not allow myself to feel judged by someone that is not actually judging me. To accept the help offered to me and not brush it off, and welcome more people into my village without feeling guilty the entire time that they are being inconvenienced as they help with the very thing they offered to help with. Or to feel weak or vulnerable when I have to ask someone for help. I can't tell you how many times I have had new moms tell me, "No, it's okay, I know you are busy with your own life, you don't have to bring us dinner. It's so sweet of you to offer but you don't have to do that," when I ask them if I can bring them a meal after they have had a new baby. When really, on the inside, they are probably screaming, "Yes!! *Feed us*!! We haven't fed ourselves properly in days!!" Even to just take the burden of thinking about food off someone's plate. It might create some extra chaos for me, but typically it leaves me with my own dinner for my family made at the same time, earlier in the day than usual, which is a bonus.

Here is the beauty in all of it: we are all just imperfect messy moms making room. I don't have it all together either to make this happen. My friends don't see that my kids might only be half dressed in the van in their car seats, they likely aren't wearing shoes and they are probably watching a movie in there. Not exactly "all put together" like it might appear. There is always sacrifice to do things for others. Yet nothing makes my heart happier than being allowed to feed new parents. It is a hard season. I want to do the little things that I can do for someone to lessen the hard in those very early days. Say yes to the help. I wish I had said yes to having someone come and hold my baby so I could nap. Those little things.

So, if you are in the throes of a new baby, whether it is your first or your fifth, let someone come so you can nap. And go nap. Do not feel guilty about not visiting. You will have more chances to visit. You need to sleep. There is not a new mom, or any mom, on earth that couldn't use more sleep. If someone is going to bless you with a nap, *take the nap.*

3.

The First Three Months

There were plenty of reasons, before kids, that I did not think it was going to be hard. I had been babysitting since I was eleven. I used to take care of five kids when I was twelve and I kept them all alive. I had been snuggling babies, changing diapers, teaching Sunday school, working in the nursery at church, and the list goes on, from as early as anyone would let me. Plus, I was a registered nurse with a specialty in emergency. Surely, if I could keep humans alive, I could handle a newborn. Right?

Wrong! I suppose I was not totally wrong. I did keep my baby alive, fed, loved, and cared for. However, it was not nearly as easy as I was expecting it to be. One would think that after realizing how hard it was just to *grow* this human, and that before he was the size of a pencil eraser he was wreaking havoc on my body, I should have been more aware of how misinformed I already was about motherhood. But I went into it with this assumption that I would be great at it. I was going to be an amazing mother. I sit here now on the eve of that first baby's seventh birthday party chuckling to myself at how different that experience was for me compared to what I imagined it would be.

Now, I kind of waffle between sharing with new first-time moms to be prepared for it to be much harder than they expect it to be, and not wanting to come across as that person that ruins the mood. The Debbie Downer. That person that comes up to you and tells you how horrific their birth was, and plants every horrible scenario you never thought of in your head days or weeks before you are about to have this baby. I never want to be that person. However, I also want to share with women that this is not going to be easy so that when it is not, they do not feel like there is something wrong with them, or that they are failing as a new mom.

The more I talked with moms and shared openly about my experiences, the more I saw the relief on their faces, and the more I realized that we are all longing to know that we are not alone. There is so much that is amazing about being a mom, and so much that tests you to the core of your being. All those Instagram- and Facebook-worthy posts about the dreaminess of motherhood and how it feels to drink in the smell of your newborn (I once heard it described as "New babies smell like unicorn tears") and to bask in all the glory are not wrong or untrue, but that is not the day-to-day in the trenches. It is okay to cry. To wonder what the heck you were thinking when you decided to embark on the journey of motherhood. To wonder when, if ever, you are going to sleep again and to feel hopeless and desperate at that thought. To have moments where your baby won't stop crying and you will carefully but firmly place them in a safe place and back away slowly. That you had this thought in your head at least once, but maybe every day or every week, that you suddenly understand why someone can shake their baby. Then, when you get to the edge of yourself and you feel like you just cannot do this for another minute, your sweet baby will do something new. They will smile at you, or giggle. Your heart will melt and you will be able to carry on.

I want every mom to know that you are *not* alone in this. You are not the first mom that felt like they failed or that had to step away from your baby so that you didn't do something that you regretted. I literally have a lump in my throat and tears rolling down my cheeks as I remember this season. So much joy and so much that was hard happened in those first months. It can be so lonely. It does not feel acceptable to tell people that you have these thoughts sometimes, or that you are struggling. That you don't feel unending joy at being a mom.

Dear mommas, please remember that in this season, you are operating in superhuman strength. Most new moms aren't sleeping for more than two to four hours at a time. For some, even less. This is totally abnormal at any other time in your life. You have significant hormone changes happening as your body readjusts to not being pregnant. Your whole world has been changed. Where you used to have the freedom to do whatever you wanted, whenever you wanted, life has been reduced to feeding a baby every three hours. Some babies take almost an hour to complete feeding and then you want to play for a little while before nap time. Hopefully your baby likes to nap, but sometimes you win the baby-that-hates-to-nap lottery, so you spend the entire nap time battling to get them to sleep, which may or may not be on you. If they sleep on you, you don't dare move a muscle or they will wake up. Then it is time to do it all over again. You can't remember the last time you showered or fed yourself, never mind doing anything else. Then, when you finally get a spare moment, you have somehow accumulated an exorbitant amount of laundry that you had better wash, because you are out of onesies and sleepers.

None of this adds up to the bliss that you may have been expecting when you dreamed of bringing this new life home. Yet, it just does not seem like the right thing to do to voice out loud how you are feeling. Then when people ask you about how amazing it is, you smile and comment on how sweet your baby is, how you never knew how much love you could have for a person and you tell them what amazing and adorable milestones they are hitting, while pulling out your phone at the same time to show them the hundreds of cute photos you have taken every single day. These are not lies. Not at all. But it often can leave you with this lonely ache inside your heart at times, because you want it all to feel like those sweet moments—but you just feel so desperate for some good sleep and time to yourself.

We are also bombarded with advice. From total strangers in the grocery stores to well meaning friends and family, plus everyone in between. Some will be helpful, some will be outright offensive, and other stuff will fall somewhere in the middle. But what do we do with all of it? This person sleep trains and that person co-sleeps. Some say sleep training gives everyone better sleep and is better for brain development. Others say co-sleeping is better for emotional attachment. And on it goes. Every single thing you hear and do will have pros and cons. It's like life. The beauty of motherhood is that this is *your* baby. You were chosen to bring this child into the world, or if you have adopted, you were chosen to be this baby's mom. This is the divine appointment to make choices and decisions for your baby. You will not get them all right, but you will do your best. Part of your best is doing what feels right for you. The things that line up with your values, beliefs, and even your personality.

For us, I did a sleep training method for my kids. I never slept well if they were in my bed. In fact, I barely even fell asleep. I used to even wake up curled up with a pillow, and my baby safely nestled in his or her own crib, and I would literally freak out because I was sure I was cuddling my baby and I had smothered him or her.

It didn't work for me. I needed the space, too. I loved to snuggle, cuddle and hold those babies and attach to them, but I also felt like I needed space or I started to feel insane. That was me. Other moms absolutely love the closeness of co-sleeping. The attachment feelings of being close together. Not having to get up in the night to nurse their child. The amazing feelings of security and closeness, all mingled together. That mom would probably not sleep with her baby in another room because she would be scared of not hearing them, or of the baby feeling lonely and scared. The beauty of it is that you get to do what resonates inside of you. Do what allows you to feel the peace of your choice, and to feel like you are showing up as the mom that you believe your baby needs. There are some parents that will probably do it both ways, depending on their babies and how they respond to either method of sleeping. It is not someone else's place to judge your choice. If you are feeling like you are drowning in decisions of what is right and what is wrong and you do not know what to do, just stop for a moment. Give yourself some space, and just think through what feels right for you.

As a person of faith, I choose to pray in these situations. I bet that if you allow the voices to slip away and you give yourself the space to trust the intuition given to you to care for your child, you will know what you need to do for your sake and for the sake of any or all of your children. Lean into it with confidence. Feel free to politely decline future advice on this situation, and let people know that you have made the right choice for yourself and your baby.

I would suspect that there is not often another time or season in life where a woman is as sleep deprived as in the first three to six months of motherhood, if not longer. You are literally *never* getting a solid amount of good restful sleep for an extended amount of time. In fact, often you aren't even getting any sleep to make note of. A nap here and there. Moms that had those sweet babies that cried for months on end, bless you. Just bless you for making it through. Honestly, even as I write this, I shudder at the very thought of what that would be like. Mine had their bouts of evening crying and long days where they were cranky and fussy, and those days felt unbearable. I remember having one such day, and someone said to me, "I bet he is colicky." All I remember saying was, "I'm pretty sure you should never say that in front of a person with a truly colicky baby," because even in that moment, I knew I did not have one of those babies that never stopped crying. I think there is a special reward for the parents that made it through. That is the stuff that is beyond superhuman! In those days where I had a fussy, gassy baby, I felt like I would pay any money for anything that was going to help. Gripe water, belly massage, and a lot of desperate prayers to just make it stop. I feel all that emotion course through my body just in remembrance of some of those times.

For those of you in those trenches today, right now, I want to hug you, feed you and bring you a warm drink. I want you to know that you will survive. You may not feel like it right now, but you will. And in the meantime, the next person that happens across your path when your baby is fed, if you are the sole milk provider and it must come from your actual body or your baby will not take a bottle from anyone but you, then once you have fulfilled that duty for your child, you lay that baby into the hands of the first person that is safe and capable, and you go have a shower. A nice hot one where you turn up music, or a podcast, or an audiobook, or maybe even just some loud white noise so you cannot hear the crying, and you stand in the shower until the water gets cold. I promise you that your baby will be fine.

You absolutely must find little sanctuaries for yourself in order to get through this season. If you do not have that capable adult, and you do not feel safe holding your baby because the anger is welling up inside of you and you are not sure what you will do, walk to the bassinette or the crib, lay them down, and walk away. This feels like you have failed as a mom. It feels terrible inside. This is the bravest thing you could ever do for the sake of your baby. This is choosing to be the very best mom you can be in this moment for your child. It will not feel like it. I promise you that. But sometimes feelings lie to us. Know in your head that you just won at the mom game. You just chose the absolute best for your baby. Even if they are screaming right now. You were aware enough to make that choice. Well done, sweet friend, well done.

Honestly, as I write this book, I am three and a half years removed from those first three months. But we got a puppy a few weeks ago. Don't worry if you are in those trenches right now and you instantly saw red when you thought I was going to dare go there and compare that season to a puppy; I am not. But what I was not expecting was that this puppy just brought up a whole lot of hard feeling. In those early months I suffered from postpartum depression. It was *hard* a lot of days. I had three kids in less than three and a half years, and many days we just barely made it through the day and we cried together in a big pile on the kitchen floor, at least once. The puppy brought back those feelings of never accomplishing anything when I had to take her outside at least once every hour to train her. The constantly meeting the need of a person (or three) and never finishing a thought, a job, a project, or even a piece of toast. That deep sense of having completely lost who you are and wondering if you are ever going to feel normal again. Every time you might have five minutes of time you do not know what to do with yourself because you have *so much to do*. The exhaustion and the hormone shifts are a perfect storm of feeling completely and totally overwhelmed. Yet, you put on a happy face for people. You learn how to make it look like this is so amazing. You put up the adorable Instagram pictures. I think part of this is that we are trying to convince ourselves. And part of it is the social expectations on us to love the heck out of motherhood, because it would be weird to say that some days you think your baby is a total monster and you don't know what you were thinking when you thought this was a good idea? Yeah. That does *not* make a great Instagram and Facebook feed at all.

Friend. Let me tell you something. I see you. With greasy hair, smelling like sour milk and you have no idea when you showered last, sitting on the floor crying with your baby. I see you grasping at those moments of intense love for your baby when you stare at them finally sleeping and they look so peaceful and you remember why you did this. I see you when you think bad thoughts in your head about the decision to have kids. I see you crawling up the stairs at bedtime thinking about how desperately you need a full night's sleep but you know that if you are lucky you will get a couple of hours, and how desperate that can feel inside to wonder how long this will last. I see you looking in the mirror at your body in disappointment that you were not one of the lucky ones who had a flat stomach a month after giving birth, and you still feel like you look seven months pregnant and when you are pulling handfuls of hair out in the shower while your hormones try and readjust themselves, and you fear you might end up bald after this. I see you trying to be intimate with your partner when you feel anything but desirable and you accidentally shoot a stream of milk across the bed at him and, in your horror, you don't know if you should burst out laughing or cry your face off.

I feel your feelings and I am here to tell you that you are going to be okay. You are going to survive. You will sleep again, probably never as good as you did before kids but it's amazing when you begin to feel like you can cope again. You are doing an amazing job while doing things that are superhuman. You are not alone in these feelings. I for one, am sitting here typing this, crying all the tears for your heart right now, because I know it is fragile and tired. Go, look at your sleeping baby (the next time they sleep), breath in their sweet smell and let it wash over you like a drug. You've got this. And if you have already made it through, well done.

4.

Postpartum Depression

The most recent statistics from 2018/2019 in Canada report that 23 percent of postpartum women report symptoms of depressive illness. It is a heavy topic, but one that must be addressed. In Canada we have amazing public health nurses that follow women in the postpartum phase. They carefully explained baby blues for me, especially with my first. Signs to watch for. To be aware that this is normal, especially as our hormones are in massive flux and we are in this almost inhumane season of sleep deprivation. It would be normal to feel a little bit low but to be aware. I heard the nurses and understood what they said. Then, I did not really dwell on it. I had no history of depression or anxiety, and wasn't this supposed to be one of the most beautiful and miraculous seasons of your life? The long-awaited child that you have dreamed of. Why would you get depressed?

As I said, I like to call baby number one "the world rocker." Each subsequent child adds to the load, changes the dynamic, and adds to the responsibility, but by then you already know what is coming. You have already adjusted your routines to factor in nap times, diaper change times, bed times, snack and feeding times, and all the other intangibles. You know that you need 1.5 million extra minutes to get out the door with babies around, and that they will poop through their cutest outfit before anyone ever gets to see it. Date nights, going to the movies, and all the time you had with your partner are now much trickier. You cannot remember the last time you both just had a lazy Saturday morning where you woke on your own schedule, snuggled, kissed, lingered and enjoyed all the time in the world with no schedule. Those days, when you rolled out of bed to either make breakfast together in limited attire, or you showered together and then headed out for a leisurely brunch and enjoyed time together, are already a thing of the past. But baby number one—as much as you think you are prepared, there is no way to be fully prepared for what is coming. And it rocks your world.

Everyone has a different story. Some have an incredible support system, while others live far away from all their people they would rely on. Others may have really hard dynamics with family. Postpartum depression is not selective. You can suffer even with the most supportive people around you and it is *not* your fault. Hormones are not balanced, and it is making your brain unhealthy. There is a point where you are not going to just "get over" this by getting enough sleep (and when is that ever going to happen in those early days?), getting enough exercise, enough food, or enough support. Sometimes you need something more. You need help. This is not weakness, it is healthy. This is *brave*. I am not here to tell you what is the best course of action for you. There are different options. But seeking professional help is key. Do not let anyone tell you that you just need to do things better or show up differently, or get bogged down by the advice of others. Find someone you trust; someone that is qualified to help you make the best plan for you to get better.

I had an amazing husband. I had family and friends around me and other new moms to hang out with. We had a church family that fed us for the first month and a work family that also provided meals. I think we would have starved in that first month if it was not for the care and concern of others to show up with food! But as time went by and I had a baby that did not like to nap, and I was a person that *needed* my time to myself, which is kind of laughable as a brand-new mom, I felt things start spiralling.

Looking back at that season much later, I realize how crazy I got. I did not see it and no one else really said anything if they saw it, but when my baby was three weeks old, I started what I called "nap boot camp." Now I cringe, looking back. Three weeks old and I thought this kid needed a schedule! *I* needed him to have a schedule. He didn't sleep on me and he didn't sleep in a crib half the time, and this left me with an awake baby in my arms almost all the time and I did not realize how poorly I was coping. I would drop him in my husband's arms at the end of the day and say I needed someone to take him. My husband felt like I was ambushing him. I am sure I was not nice in my delivery. In hindsight, we probably both needed to come at each other with a whole lot more grace than we did. But we were both new to this and in many ways, we were both drowning. I'm sure I was hard to like for much of that time and he probably thought his wife was broken. This made him stay a bit later at work each night. I felt unsupported and like I could barely accomplish anything, let alone make supper, and then with him coming home later, I was angrier and angrier. No one was meeting my needs or expectations ever.

Then we started to yell at each other. For us, this was new and different and absolutely the worst way to actually interact with each other. I had learned long before to actually try to take as much emotion *out* of our conversation for the sake working out an issue, and this was a completely destructive way that we were showing up for each other. In some cases of postpartum depression, moms do not attach to the baby and that might seem more obvious. In our case, I was still attached to him, aside from the crazy sleep training where I would cry for the whole nap right along side him. But I was just so angry with everyone else. As well as hurt, and very anxious.

One morning I was driving two hours to visit family. I wanted to shower, and my husband was still home before work. In my mind, he would automatically know that I would rather shower in peace and he could entertain our child for ten minutes while I showered. As it turns out, he does not read minds. A little aside that will make your relationship better: Stop waiting for your partner to read your mind. It is not going to happen. Swallowing your pride and spelling it out, even if it hurts, usually results in everyone's needs being better met. So, I stomped around and got the bouncy chair and put it in the bathroom and seethed while I showered. Then he came up and asked me what my problem was. I can see it all playing out before my eyes even now. He said those words and I saw red. I started yelling and he stormed out. Probably the one and only time we have ever had a yelling match with each other and he literally walked out on me without a word. I cried and cried. I drove and cried. I stopped half way to nurse the baby. It was like in that moment that God opened my eyes to the awareness that this was not normal.

I don't think that everyone has this moment. Oftentimes, you may not have this insight and you need to trust someone else to help share it with you. It will probably make you livid, because that is how postpartum depression works. But please, if you are in this place, if this is hitting too close to home, let them speak truth into your life. Let them help you. Mad or not. You will be well sooner, and you will realize how desperately you needed help.

There I sat. Completely aware that this was way past baby blues or just being a new mom. This was me in some of the darkest days of my life and I was drowning in the hurt, pain, anger, and anxiety of it all. It was ruining my marriage and keeping me from truly enjoying motherhood. The awareness gave me some relief. I made a doctor's appointment right there and I sent my husband a text. I probably did not apologize. I was probably still really mad. I just remember saying that I realized I was not okay, that this was not normal, and I was going to see the doctor because I was pretty sure this was postpartum depression. It was a turning point for us. He realized I was not just going to be like this forever and that his wife was not ruined. He showed up with more grace. He promised to help me more and to be more careful with my feelings.

I went to the doctor and she usually gives me options and lets me choose what I want to do. However, in this case she told me I needed medication. I am not going to spell out my whole health plan for that season. I think it is different for everyone but know this - making a plan that is best for you with someone qualified is key. I struggled to accept it because I still felt like I was not someone that struggled with depression. I felt so weak but I embraced the plan because I also wanted to be well and I knew I was so far from it. Over the first couple of weeks, I still struggled to embrace it. The medication made me feel fuzzy for the first week and I was trying so hard to convince myself that I did not need this, that I almost quit taking them. But then, slowly, I started to feel different. Better. The fog that I did not know I was in, lifted. My husband admitted he felt like his wife was returning. I was finally able to enjoy motherhood and it did not feel like it was always so hard.

Friends, motherhood is not for the faint of heart on a good day, you need to be functioning at your best to take on that beast day in and day out. So, let's band together and raise up our friends that are struggling quietly, and rally the troops to surround these women with love, grace, and support.

During my second pregnancy, we talked about postpartum depression beforehand and my doctor advised that I was higher risk for it the second time around, with my history. But she also agreed to let me just assess it as we went along. Initially, I felt pretty good. I did not feel like the second time around was as hard as the first. I was probably feeding my family within a few weeks in spite of having had my second C-section in less than two years and having a newborn and one-year-old at home, which felt like a win.

Then at three months postpartum, my symptoms hit. This was at about the same period after my first son was born, when my husband and I had that screaming match in our bedroom. The anxiety hit full force. Almost overnight, I was angry. Anxious. No one was meeting my expectations. It hit hard and fast. But thankfully, we had a plan and I went on medication almost right away, and while it took some time to really get a grip on it, we could put a name to what was happening. My husband was again gracious with me, and we managed to get it under control quickly.

Postpartum depression with baby three was just a given. My doctor did not really give me the option. And I did not want to go through that again. So, we just managed it right from about three weeks postpartum with medication. But to be honest, there was still a low at three months. That was my low spot. It might be different for everyone, but I could pinpoint it to that hormone shift around that time. Thankfully, I had also found some different natural tools to use by this time as well and I was able to support my body in multiple ways.

I do not share my health plan with you in order to tell you what you need and what your body needs. It is vital that each person works with a health professional to find the right course of action for them. There are also community resources available. In Canada, we have an excellent public health system, with nurses that are trained in perinatal care that are available to connect with you and to help you find other resources for more support. There is help out there, ready and waiting for you.

What I want each mom to take away from this chapter is that, while I already discussed that the first three months can be so hard regardless of all the emotions, for some, it feels like it is *too* hard. If it feels like you are lost and drowning, lonely and angry; this is not normal. This is beyond what you should expect in this season. Left alone and untreated, it can be catastrophic to you and your baby, and even subsequent babies. Oftentimes, pregnancy can actually put postpartum depression into remission because of that change in hormones. However, it can manifest even stronger after the next baby. You are not weak. You are so brave when you get help. You are fighting for yourself, your babies, and even your relationship—and you are a warrior. If you are struggling, please put this book down right now and tell someone. And if you have come out the other side of postpartum depression, please know how proud I am of you. It takes courage to fight your way out of the darkness, and I hope you savour the warmth of that light on your face on the other side.

5.

Let's Talk About That Body

As women, I would say there is a very small section of our population, if any, that truly embraces their body image and loves it just the way it is. We are our own worst critic. Even before kids I was never happy with my weight, my love handles, the rolls where I did not want them. My skin was not flawless. My torso is short, so shirts don't fit right. On it goes. It is a lie we believe from a young age that our bodies are not good enough. We fight to lose weight, to make changes, to do what it takes to be happier with how we look. Maybe you are at a point where you are satisfied. I hope you feel that way now, but I suspect that would be the minority of women.

Then, you get pregnant. Now you are growing a human inside of you where there was never a human before. Have you ever stopped to consider this? Have you ever stopped to consider what a miracle this is? That women have this little pear-sized organ inside our bodies that is there to house a human for nine months? And then, our bodies actually adapt around this growing human to keep functioning as they should while a baby pushes on everything in there. At first, you just get thicker around the middle. Maybe it is a tiny little bit of a bump, but mainly it just looks like your clothes do not fit right and you are at that awkward stage where people that see you wonder, but don't dare ask you if you are pregnant. Then, it finally pops out to look more of a cute little bump. You stand in the mirror sideways and stare at it with wonder and start rub your belly subconsciously, dreaming of that little person in there and who they are.

As the pregnancy progresses through the second trimester, it can be pretty awesome for some. You are feeling well and that bump is adorable and small. Personally, I felt like this was where I finally embraced my figure for what it was and what it was doing. But for many women, even in this season it can be hard to fully embrace what is happening here. It feels like the baby weight is coming on everywhere, not just where the baby is growing. Your pelvis is loosening and may be causing all kinds of sharp knifing pains that make it hard to get around properly. The baby is camped out on your bladder and you are probably never going to be free of issues from this short-term rental agreement where your bladder is concerned ever again. Let's just say your trampoline days are done. For some women, those muscles in your abdomen are pulling apart which is horribly painful. But you are growing a human! A *human being*! It can be hard with all these reminders of how your body is changing not to lose sight of the miracle that you are. Or, of the fact that without these changes that you would not be able to bring this life into the world. The strength to grow a human is so incredible.

Once you get to the third trimester, it has become a stretch to even ensure proper hygiene. Reaching things like you used to is a thing of the past. You need to do some Cirque du Soleil moves to get around that belly every time you go to the bathroom. No one talks about this! But it is a real issue! You have "cankles" instead of ankles, and have resorted to some type of slip-on shoe that is well beyond your normal size (spoiler alert: You are probably never getting your feet back into lots of those cute heels you used to wear before kids. I'm not sure what happens to your shoe size, but it is not the same after babies), and you are long past the days where you could tie your own shoes. If it is winter, you are typically inappropriately dressed, because it is hard to justify buying all new outdoor wear to accommodate this growing bump. But you are growing a human!

Then this baby comes out. On average, that is about seven or eight pounds of baby, a placenta, and a whole lot of fluid that is out (which, if your water broke on its own when you are somewhere completely inopportune like the grocery store, you will never forget just how *much* fluid that was). Now you should be feeling more normal right? You may have taken some pre-pregnancy pants to the hospital in your bag when you were about to deliver that first baby. Only to find out, with some horror in my own case, that you still looked very pregnant after the baby was out. Only, your belly is squishy now. At least that bump could be considered cute. But now you are left with this squishy mess and a massive hormone storm, bags under your eyes from the overwhelming sleep deprivation, and you are pretty sure you have never looked worse. Thankfully, our hearts are never so full of love as they are toward that baby. I think that is a gift from God to keep us going in this season. You grew a human!

This is the season where you need to remind yourself every single time you go by that mirror or see a picture, that you are a superhero. That this body that you are cringing at is nothing short of a miracle maker! You are a beautiful picture of what it means to show up selflessly for the sake of your babies, to grow them inside of you and keep them safe and cared for, for nine months. No one else got to do that job for those little humans that you grew.

You, and you alone, gave them life and *that* is nothing short of incredible. The stretch marks, maybe a C-section scar, the squishy body; these are your marks of honour. These are your war wounds for fighting for the lives of your babies. Look at them with pride. It will be a constant fight to look at them this way. I do not always look at them this way. Some days, I look at my body and I shutter and cringe and look away. But I am working at seeing it for the beauty that it is.

Let's celebrate the beauty it is to be women. Even women who have never borne children from their bodies. Some are not able to. Some do not want to. But body image remains an issue for women. Let us stop having ideals of what we should be, and just remind each other that each person is beautiful. What if you tell the next woman that you see that she is beautiful? Even if you don't know her. I guarantee, as weird and awkward as it may feel, you will make that person's day. If we did this more and criticized less, or rather, not at all, it could be revolutionary.

Sweet mommas that are cringing at your squishy bodies, maybe you are two weeks postpartum and maybe you are twenty years postpartum, I want you to look at yourself today and say "I am enough. I am beautiful. This body housed miracles, and these are all the signs and reminders of what this body has done. I am blessed to have these reminders of the privilege it is to have carried a human being, or multiple human beings in this body." You are brave, strong and remarkable.

6.

The Toddler Years

When I was getting ready to write this chapter, I thought it would be fitting to find just the right quote to talk about toddlers and what they are like. But I was laughing so hard at all of them, that I could not pick just one. However, the fact that there are so many out there highlights the fact that we are never alone in what feels like the bipolar nature of toddlers. They literally make you feel like you are going crazy at times. Yet, they are full of so much wonder and excitement about the simplest things in life that you are constantly living in this push and pull of complete and total love and devotion, and the insanity of their ever-changing personality. Every mom that combs through their "previously on this day" memories struggles with how to repost five different adorable posts without seeming annoying, because there are just so many cute ones. Sometimes I even post videos on social media for myself to see in a year or two, to be reminded of this moment. But in the trenches, it is as many women have said before us, "The days are long but the years are short." I don't think you have really arrived as a mom until you have sat in the middle of the floor somewhere and given in to the tears. Where you just sit in a heap of children, crying with them. This is a rite of passage.

These moments are not failure or weakness in any way, they are just a part of life. You will brush yourself off and keep going, but stay there as long as you need to. Chances are, the littlest in your lap will bounce back before you. They might even show some concern over your tears and flip a switch to comforting you. It is the sweetest thing and can turn a situation around in some cases. Do not feel like your kids can't see your tears. Showing your emotions and showing them how to manage them is a gift. This is part of life. The best thing we can do is have conversations very early on about our feelings and how to express them in a healthy way. Our lives will be filled with good and hard emotions, often co-existing at the same time. Teaching our kids how to manage them will set them up far better as adults to manage their feelings well. We have all been privy to an adult that acted less mature than your toddler, and it is *not* pretty. So just lean into those days, and maybe you can even have a teaching moment.

With toddlers, you will go for many days as they learn to eat and drink where you give them whatever colour cup, plate or bowl that is on top of the stack. This will be perfectly acceptable. Until the day it is not. On that day, hell hath no fury like a toddler that wanted the blue cup and got the orange one. They will throw it and pitch a fit. Refuse to eat. If it is your first, you might stand there a little shocked at this turn of events. If this is not your first, you will sigh, maybe say a word or two in your head that shall not be repeated, and you buckle down. The colour season is here. You have plenty of battles to pick, and what colour of utensils and dishes is not likely going to be one of them. For the fore-seeable future, blue is your colour. Until it is not. Some kids will hold hard and fast to one colour. But many times, you will think you are winning the day when all the blue dishes come out of the dishwasher and you are equipped and ready! Only to find out that your child's new best friend loves green and now *that* is the *only* option. All the solidarity to you in this season. If can be a long, hard, well-fought battle. You will survive, but I cannot promise it will be without any battle scars.

On top of the colour battles, many toddler freak-outs have happened over food. That same child lying on the floor weeping over how much they hate bananas could have indeed been the same child that ate three bananas for breakfast yesterday. Today, they are no longer banana fans. Or, the child who deemed appropriate that plate of toast that is crustless and cut into the shape of a dinosaur in the exact specifications that were demanded, might not want toast anymore because you took so long making it exactly the way they asked. In that time, they either came up with other ideas or they spied something that a sibling was eating that caught their attention. Now, that work-of-art piece of toast is a hard no. All the while, your cup of tea or coffee is sitting on the counter getting cold all over again for the third time. Maybe on the sixth reheat you will get a sip. Or not, because you might just end up finding it hours later, still in the microwave when you open it up to warm up the latest cup that you made yourself that went cold.

There is an emotional investment that toddlers require that can push you to the brink on many days. I wonder if part of it is that little ones are not attached to your person but it's your job to keep them alive, or ensure they are in the care of someone that will keep them alive, but they are so capable of pushing those boundaries with their curiosity at all times. You don't even have to look away for them to try something dangerous or gross, they will happily do it right in front of you. But sometimes you just cannot move fast enough. My coffee table and wide window sills all have footprints as well as handprints on them. I would turn around and someone was standing on the kitchen table. Turn to the kitchen, and a little hand is reaching up over the end of the counter to grab whatever

42

they can get their hands on. Even that sharp butcher knife you didn't push back far enough. Have you ever turned around just to see your child lifting that sharp knife up over their head, and you feel all the horror in the world as you try to force it down and calmly move towards them and not scare them into dropping it onto their own face and into their eye? My mouth goes dry just thinking about it right now. There is no impulse control and it is terrifying, not to mention emotionally exhausting.

In our home the coordination of most of the things in our life falls to me. I think that is pretty common in many homes that this is the job of moms. Just this past weekend my kids were taking apart a broken electronic device. I said to them when they got inside it, "That piece is where all the signals come into, and it coordinates all the processes and signals and makes this thing work, it's called the motherboard. For good reason." My husband is an amazing dad and he does his share of helping and caring for the kids. I am so grateful for this. However, when it comes to organizing life and making the plans for who will be where, when, how, and wearing what, with the right supplies, I am the COO of the house. This can be a lot on our brains as moms. While I was at work, I would think about them. Did they get where they were going, or did they get picked up when they were supposed to? Did their day go okay? On it goes. Our brains are largely focused on our kids. I think this remains true even as they grow, but when they are very small and unable to problem-solve a situation that is not going right and we, as moms, do not have the control when we are apart from them to make sure everything is fine, it can be an added burden to our hearts and brains.

The thing with toddlers is that we have to take them everywhere we go. Unless we have someone to watch them, but there is no leaving them behind on their own. Yet, they are the hardest to take anywhere, especially into stores. How many times have you ever ignored the fact that you are scraping the bottom of the barrel for groceries or you haven't washed your hair for days on end because you ran out of shampoo but the idea of going out to a store is just too much to bear? We have all been there. Finally, you decide you cannot hold off any longer and you pack up the kids and off you go. You prep the kids:

"Do we touch things without asking?"

"Yesssssssss…"

"Excuse me? Do we touch things without asking?"

"Nooooooo…"

"Thank you. If everyone is good and no one touches things without asking, then we will get a treat that you can have when we are done."

Off you go. Wherever the first child wants to sit in the cart, any other kids also will want that exact location. After a bit of a fight, everyone is riding someone on or in the cart. This is completely counterproductive to actually filling the cart with what you need but at the same time, they are contained. The struggle is real as to whether you buy less and keep them there, or eventually pull them out to fill your cart. If you pile things around them, they will eventually want to get out anyway and they will stand up at the worst possible time, sending things flying in all directions. You quickly try to grab them as they throw themselves out of the cart; all the while, some disapproving person without kids is watching the whole thing and you are sure they are thinking about how dangerous it is for kids to be standing in shopping carts, and what a bad mom you are.

Now, everyone is situated with two feet on the ground and they start "helping." This is similar to being in a video game trying not to hit people, displays, and anything else in your way while the toddlers help push the cart. That is, until they see something that demands their attention and they run off to touch it and everything around it, to which you start to say, "Remember, we talked about not touching things before we got here?" on repeat at least one hundred times.

Then the requests for everything they see start coming in. This starts to set the mood to a high probability of a meltdown. This is now the point of your shopping experience where it is very possible that you will be faced with a crying child, where you must either abandon the cart and carry them out kicking and screaming, or shove them in the front of the cart and push it around with the feral child crying as if nothing is happening here. Or, if it isn't a melting-down child, someone will need to pee and you are about as far away from the bathroom as you can get, and they are on the other side of the cashiers where you ideally would pay for your cart of groceries before accessing the bathrooms. Then you promise yourself that you will go shopping at 9:00 p.m. next time and your only companion will be a hot latte that you sip as you wander the aisles in peace. When online grocery shopping became a new thing, and then it went even farther to grocery delivery, I may have shed a tear of thankfulness and gratitude.

In those moments when a child is having a full-blown tantrum in the aisle, it seems like someone comes along and feels like they want to remind us that we will miss this one day. Umm, no. I actually *won't* miss this. I will never miss this. I will never miss the embarrassment of a tantruming child in the grocery store where I cannot decide if I need to abandon my cart, or carry on while this continues because we desperately need the groceries. I will absolutely not miss *this*. I will miss the moments where they are sweetly smiling at me in the cart and saying hi to everyone in the store and people are telling me that my child is so sweet and well mannered. I will miss that. Not this. I never will. For the most part people mean well, I know that. It would just be nice if we could maybe just offer some support and a helping hand instead of advice in those hard moments, wouldn't it? Sometimes I carry a few five-dollar gift cards for Starbucks in my purse so that in those moments I can give one to a poor mom that is dying inside and tell her to grab herself a coffee on the drive home. To remind her that she is not alone, every mom has been there, and she is still doing a great job even though it does not feel like it.

I have one toddler that turns into a kitty as soon as we hit the doors of any store. She starts meowing and wants to crawl around on all fours. Sometimes I let her. If her hands are on the floor, they aren't touching and grabbing things. She tends to stay closer this way too. I do choose carefully where I let this happen, and ensure that I have hand sanitizer in my purse as well for when she stands back up. Some people think it is cute. But I can tell from the looks that others give her, and me, they think it's weird, gross, and kind of ridiculous that I'm allowing this to go on. I have learned not to care. She has an amazing immune system, she is happy, and she is not touching things she shouldn't be. She is also not crying, fussing, or making this harder than it has to be. Therefore, we are winning the day.

Whatever you do to the win the day with toddlers, kudos to you! People can save their judging glances for someone else. Put on your blinders, engage with your kitty and chances are, your shopping experience will be more fun for both of you. Your kitty will make memories where you let her be creative and have fun while you were out. I also talk to my kitty while we are shopping. I actually call her sometimes, "Here kitty, kitty, come over here please. Stay close." And she does it. Bonus points if your kitty chose her own clothes that day and she is wearing four patterns, a dress over pants with two different socks, and she did her own hair too. Your job is to embrace her independence, make sure she knows she is beautiful and take a picture for the wedding slide show! And to know that you are awesome.

The sleep deprivation changes from the newborn season, but it doesn't go away in the toddler years. I'm actually not entirely sure if it ever does. Seven years later and we are still in the trenches of it over here. My first child actually found his thumb at two months old and started fully sleeping through the night. I distinctly remember talking to a friend quite some time later about her son (our babies were only a few weeks apart), and she told me that almost a year later, he still wasn't sleeping through the night. In my mind I thought, how do you *live* like that? That's not even possible and why aren't you doing something about this? I sort of judged the whole situation in that moment, but my time was quickly coming to fully understand what this was like. Kids have a way of making you eat your words (and thoughts) every single time.

My next one didn't sleep through the night for eight or nine months and my third one didn't sleep through the night for almost a year. Even then, they weren't consistent. Once you have more, they basically have a team conference before bed and plan their attack. "How can we ensure that we maximize the night? You take a turn at 11:00 p.m., just as mom is falling into a deep sleep. This will ensure that she startles awake and is then awake for a significant period of time after she gets back into bed. I'll take the 1:00 a.m. - 2:00 a.m. slot, and this will be when she's in her deepest sleep. She will stumble around, feel anxious about getting back to her bed, give me everything I demand in the quickest fashion she can, and then stumble back to her room. She may or may not stay awake after that. Then the last kid takes the 4:00 a.m. - 5:00 a.m. slot. This is where she is kind of waking up and we have the best chance of her not being able to fully fall back to sleep before morning, and she will toss and turn. By now she will have had a terrible sleep and we will be up for the day! She will now be at our mercy to survive the day on very little sleep and she will give us extra shows, more treats, and probably, if we play our cards right through the day, we will get popcorn and a show too close to supper so we are not hungry for our supper and we will not have to eat whatever she managed to scrape together. Okay guys, this plan is perfect. Let's do it!" This can go on for years, I have discovered.

Toddlers are intense. They are irrational, unpredictable, and kind of gross. They will never miss the opportunity to get to the top of a play structure in a fast food restaurant and find the nearest "window" to call you from, only to lick the window ledge while calling, "Hiiiii Mommmmm!" from up there, while you shout, "Stop putting your mouth on that thing!!" back at them in the most endearing exchange. Yet, they are also the most innocent and sweet that they will ever be. The love us with their whole self and just when you think you can't go on, they will run up and wrap their chubby little arms around your neck and say, "I love you mommy," which is the absolute sweetest little gift you have ever received.

Let us come together as moms and stand in solidarity with other toddler moms. Maybe you just offer a simple "I see you and I know how this feels" when you see a mom in the middle of a freak-out in the store. Or, you can offer to stand by the grocery cart when you hear her child announcing to the entire grocery store that he "needs to poop right now!!" Perhaps you are past this season in life and your kids are in school, but there is a mom in your neighborhood with littles and you could offer to take the kids to the park or walk around the block or even just play in their back yard while she has a little break and drinks a cup of hot coffee or has a power nap. Or maybe you make twice as much dinner for your family and let her know you will drop it off when it is ready.

Sweet moms in the toddler trenches, I get you. It all passes in what feels like forever and the blink of an eye, all at the same time. You long for more sleep and to pee alone. You are over-touched many days, and yet you can't stop hugging and kissing those cheeks all at the same time. It feels like you are going crazy when you give them exactly what they asked for but it isn't right, and you have no idea what is wrong. Letting them "help" can be more work when it ends up making twice the mess and you aren't sure if they have completely botched the whole meal by accident. You want to help them be independent but also just want to do it yourself for the ease of getting something done quickly. You long for the opportunity to think for more than a moment without someone interrupting. Yet, there are those moments where they snuggle in and fall asleep on your chest that are so rare. The feeling of that little hand sliding into yours by their own choice releases all the feel-good endorphins, or when they put those chubby hands on your cheeks and tell you they love you and give you a slobbery kiss.

You are constantly stuck in this space of wanting to keep them small and rush them through this stage. Torn between the weight of hating the season when you feel pushed to the edge of your sanity, and feeling the deep ache in your chest when you look at them with all the love you feel and think that this time is short and slipping away too fast. Do your best to lean into the good moments. To sit and savour them. When your toddlers come into your room much too early and you want to send them back to their beds to teach them that they need to wait until morning to get up, maybe just pull back the covers and let them snuggle. If the to-do list is long and you struggle with getting it done but your toddler says, "Please come snuggle me, Mommy," let yourself put the list aside and scoop them up and hold them close. People will tell you all the time that you are going to miss these days. You will. But they always seem to tell you these things when you are a hot mess in public somewhere or you are telling some harrowing story about your toddler.

Like the grocery store tantrums, you are not going to miss everything about these days. So much of mothering toddlers can be about survival. For you and for them. Finding your little ways to regain your sanity is key. Maybe yours is to put them in the car and hit up the closest drive-thru. Do it. Maybe you found a friend and you guys have a code word for when you need to hand over your toddlers for a little break. Do it. Maybe you need to make hot chocolate and popcorn and put the kids in laundry baskets with blankets and put on a movie. Do it. What you don't need to do is to live with the feeling of guilt or failure that you are struggling to love this stage every minute, that you are not doing the right things and your kids aren't going to turn out right. That does not serve you well, and it is lies to steal your joy. You are a great mom and you are completely normal to feel all these things. There is not a mother out there that breezed through the toddler years. You are a superhero and you have the sweetest fan club in the world right there in your own home. Those toddlers love you more than life itself, Momma. You are their whole world.

7

Personal Space...
What Personal Space?

"Hi Mommy. Why are you in your room? I came up here to be with you because I knew you would be lonely without me. I knew you would be missing me and I didn't want that. So I came up here to be with you. Aren't you happy about that? Why do you have tears? Because you missed me?"

Then she wrapped her little arms around my neck and gave me a big squeeze, told me that she loved me and said not to worry, that she would keep me company and I wouldn't have to be alone.

When I did the Myers-Briggs personality test, I rated 51 percent introvert and 49 percent extrovert. It allows me to fill my cup both in a group of people, as well as at home in the quiet of my own space. I had an amazing run of roommates all through my college years. But once I finished university, I got my own place and lived alone. I vowed I was never going back unless I got married, and then I would let him in. For six years I got to savour my very own space. No one messed it up. It was tidy almost all the time, and clean too! Those two things were able to co-exist, and it was glorious. When I wanted to be with people, I invited them over or I went out and hung out with friends. When I wanted to be alone, I went inside, locked the door, and did not talk to a soul. About five days into my honeymoon, I had a bit of a panic attack and thought, "I have not been alone for what feels like even ten minutes, what have I done?" I probably laugh about that now more than my husband does, but that was where we had to start having the really honest conversations in our marriage. To be honest, if there is one person I want to spend almost all my time with, it is him. So, it worked out well, but my introverted self was just a tad concerned about how this was going to look moving forward.

Fast forward to kids a couple of years later. We had found a good balance as a couple, to meet our needs. Then we had our first child. Suddenly, I went from time alone to having someone not only in my presence day and night, but also needing to feed off of me every three hours, if not almost continuously at times. He was so needy! You might think, "What else were you expecting?" Honestly, I did not really give it much thought before that moment. There I was, exhausted after more than twenty-four hours of labour followed by a middle of the night C-section, so in love, sore, and connected to tubes, that it was hard to even figure out how to manage this baby. Then I realized that, for the foreseeable future, I would not be alone. I'm sure I cried about this on day three. It was a huge eye-opener for me.

I believe this is one of the many reasons that God gives us this overwhelming unconditional love for this small human being. The momma instinct to love and care for them better than anyone else ever could, is both the superpower and, at times, the kryptonite of motherhood. It allows us to be completely consumed with this person. This is where moms become plagued by the insanity of feeling like you need to nap when your babies do, but you also want to stay awake and just stare at how sweet they are when they are sleeping, because it's so amazing. There is basically nothing rational about a new mom. It is the incredible mix of so hard and so incredible all rolled together in this unexplainable, beautiful hot mess.

The days of doing anything alone are over for awhile. In fact, the days of even having the use of two hands for anything are gone for awhile. You suddenly become a master at peeing with a baby, doing up your pants one-handed, and cooking and eating with one hand. It is actually remarkable how adaptable we become. Some babies love the carrier or the sling and this provides a little bit more freedom, but my first two kids hated it. I managed to figure out how to put them up on my shoulder and tuck them in under my chin if I needed two hands for something. To this day, when I see a mom trying to eat with her baby in her arms, I ask if I can hold the baby and let her have the freedom to just sit and eat a meal with a knife and a fork like a normal adult. It's the little things.

Then, just to complicate things even a little more, the baby inevitably needs to nurse right as dinner is ready. I cannot even remember how many times I sat at the table nursing a baby while I ate my dinner. There are moments when, as a new mom, it can feel like life as you know it is over. For me, personally, this was one of them. That season did end and now I keep my shirt on for every meal again, but I remember very clearly the emotions and feelings of that season.

Every mom is different and the whole act of nursing a baby is different for each mom. Some women just adore that stage. They lean heavily into it and find so much joy while doing it. For some, nursing comes easy, the baby stays under the cover, or the moms are so good at latching their baby on and making it all so discrete that you would hardly even notice a baby is nursing. Others just don't even care if they are exposed, and that is okay too. I struggled with the whole concept of nursing. I loved that I was able to give nourishment to my baby, as well as the bonding and the intimacy of it. But it was hard. I was not discrete. My babies hated a nursing cover and it was a full-blown production just to nurse them. Honestly, I did not love it. No one told me that every time my milk let down it was going to briefly feel like someone stabbed a knife in my nipples. Every single time. That I was going to have these soggy pieces of cloth shoved in my bra all the time or I was going to be a leaky mess everywhere. No one else was going to be able to do this job for me if I needed a nap or a break, or I just didn't want to do it today. It was not going to be like it was when I didn't have kids and didn't want to cook, and we ordered pizza or went out for dinner. There was no one else. It was just me. I had a love-hate relationship with that feeling. On one hand, it made me feel special and needed. On the other hand, it made me feel trapped and kind of crazy sometimes. I was able to pump a bit of milk for my babies so that I had the odd time where I might be able to get out for a few hours. This always felt amazing, until I missed that feed. Then I became so engorged that all I could think of was getting home and latching that baby which took away a bit of the enjoyment of being out.

Once you have your first child, your personal space is no longer your own. Whether you have one or more, someone else came along and rented that space that was not actually up for rent. Then comes the day when they start to crawl and ultimately walk. Now they can actually follow you every where. You can try and lock yourself in the bathroom, but they will lie on the floor shouting by the door with their small hand shoved underneath it, or better yet, moaning for you like a dying animal and making it seem like you have certainly left them to fend for themselves for the last ten hours or so, rather than the last ten seconds where you thought you would just quickly pee alone without having a toddler climb up and demand a hug and a cuddle, mid-pee.

I distinctly remember trying to ninja into the bathroom when my oldest was about two and a half years old and I had my period and wanted a few moments of privacy. I thought I had managed to be fairly discreet about the whole thing and just as I sat down on the toilet, the door immediately burst open and he came rushing in and shouted, "Don't worry Mom, I can help!!" He threw open the cabinet doors under the sink and started pulling out a wide variety of feminine hygiene products, asking me what I needed and what he could help with. I think it was one of the most horrifying moments of my motherhood life at that point.

There have certainly been many more horrifying moments since then. Like the time he found the backing of a panty liner in a bucket in the garage that my husband had dumped all the bathroom garbage in, to dump for garbage day, and he ran after me down the street when his little brother was on the loose waving it in the air, shouting, "Mommm, here's that thing you put over your penis!!"

With my first baby I was at least able to escape to a quiet rocking chair alone to nurse. With my second, my older child actually enjoyed perching himself up on my shoulders while I nursed the baby. So now, even more of my bubble was filled with small people. There were twice as many needs to be filled. Twice as many boys that felt like they should, at the very least, have their hand down my shirt at any given time. As well as twice as much love. That is what we are supposed to say as moms, right? In those moments all of our emotional resources can feel completely tapped. It is hard to hold on to the love when you feel like you are over-touched. When the baby is getting much of the attention, then the older one steps up their demands. It can feel overwhelming. It is okay not to enjoy every minute of it.

Much to my surprise, when my second child was nine months old, I got pregnant with my third. So, when she arrived, I had a not quite three-and-a-half-year-old, an eighteen-month-old and a brand-new baby. I cried when I initially found out I was pregnant again. I did not feel ready. I was craving space, and maybe a sangria in the summer. I was struggling with my emotions and postpartum feelings. The constant clinging to me was hard for me to take at all times. I am actually a very affectionate person, but I was feeling maxed out.

When we first got married, we read the book *The Five Love Languages* by Gary Chapman. The premise is that you give and receive love in five primary ways, and that you will have a dominant where you feel the most loved when someone that cares for you "speaks" your love language. For example, I love words of affirmation, meaning I feel the most loved when my husband speaks words of encouragement and love to me. His is physical touch, so he feels the most loved if I hold his hand in the car, or rub his back in church, or just generally make physical contact in our day-to-day life. Physical touch was my close second right after we got married. I took the quiz again after I had three kids and it was at the bottom of the list. I actually love hugging, loving, and kissing my kids and my husband. However, in this season I feel like there are limits and I have, at times, exceeded them. Sometimes I am out-touched. I have to be very aware of this, for my husband's sake, so that he does not feel unloved by me.

Loving your partner the way *they* need to feel loved will be instrumental to both of you showing up for each other and your kids the best. It will strengthen your relationship with each other, but it is not easy. In fact, you will feel like they should just understand why you aren't speaking their love language in this season, but sometimes they don't. I find myself in this place often as a wife and a mom. It can, at times, be hard work to touch my husband when he comes in the door if I have been covered in clingy kids and crying babies all day. We go through periods where I rarely focus on giving him some of my attention and affection, but I also notice that we are not as connected as parents in those periods either. When we both work harder to show up speaking each other's love language, the day-to-day feels a little easier.

Be real and honest with your partner. You need time and space to yourself. You need some mom time-outs. Assure them that you will show up better for everyone if you can take some time. Walk away and do *not* feel guilty for it. When you do walk away, allow yourself the opportunity to take some deep breaths, take time, drink a cup of tea or do whatever you love. A few minutes will not always fix it, but take enough time so that you can, at the very least, show up as even a little bit better version of yourself. This shows your partner and your kids that sometimes you will step away, but you will come back better able to respond. To love. To dig just a bit deeper to make it to bedtime.

For the solo parents, or the ones that have partners working away for periods of time, first of all, I think you are rock stars. It may take some extra creativity to take time for yourself. Chances are high that you are so used to doing this alone, it is hard to ask for help or to admit that you need someone else to step in so that you can step away. You are not weak to ask for help. To send your kids to the neighbour's house for a little while, or put on a show, or allow some screen time even if they had too much TV time earlier. Sometimes, for the sake of everyone's wellbeing, we need to do what it takes in those moments to step out and take a deep breath and regroup.

There will be times when you need to reclaim your personal space for the sake of your sanity, yet there will be *many* times where you do not have the luxury. At the end of the day, our children need us. We love this and struggle with it in a weird sort of yin and yang that hangs over us for all of motherhood. We need space and want them to snuggle with us, all at the same time. We want them to grow up fast and stay small forever. It is a defining characteristic of motherhood, that we are always in conflict with ourselves of what we truly want and need. In these moments where we are being bombarded with littles, try to lean into it. Pick them up. Hold them close. Bring them fully into your space with intention, rather than just that peripheral touching that happens all the time. I find that in these moments they feel seen, touched, heard and cared for, and that closeness seems to release some type of endorphins in our brains that allow that closeness to break through the feeling of wanting to just pull away and not be touched. By the grace of God, often in those exact moments where I wanted to push them away, tell them to go play or just say no, when instead I lean into just putting down all the things, these are the moments when my kids put their little faces close to mine and their sticky, chubby little hands on my cheeks and say, "Mommy, I love you." Cue all the mom tears. The gratitude that you let them up into your lap. Your cup can feel like it suddenly went from dry to overflowing and you want to remember this moment for the rest of time. Stay completely present for it. Resist the urge to start thinking about what if I had not said yes? What if I had just kept doing my list of things to do and missed this? Do not go there. Just be completely present, grateful and filled up.

Just tonight, I was wiping the table, kind of lost in my thoughts after supper and my littlest was supposed to be getting ready for bed. But she informed me that she was still hungry. I fairly abruptly told her, "Then you should have eaten more supper," and kind of dismissed her. She was supposed to be upstairs and this was my quiet time to myself. She persisted and I asked if she wanted a carrot, to which she was delighted. So, I figured she must actually be hungry. We have been working on her using the peeler herself, and carrots are proving to be a great learning vegetable to peel. She was standing on the stool chatting with me about me how I was doing my job wiping the table and she was doing her job peeling carrots and we were both acting like moms. Then I hear this little voice behind me say, "I'm a great mom, but *you* Mommy, you are strong and brave, and are a great mommy. You are so good at that Mommy; you are great at wiping the table. I can't wait to be a mommy like you." Just ten minutes earlier, I had been thinking that she was infringing on my time alone in peace to clean up the kitchen and not have to help anyone, or be pulled in ten directions, or mediate a fight. That sweet little three-year-old soul blessed my heart so much. She can be the one that sucks me dry sometimes, and yet she fills my cup more than almost any human on this planet, all in the same span of time. She can interrupt me so many times, and on that very last "Mommy?" And I say, "What??" just a little too sharply, she will say, "I just love you and I want to keep you forever."

Moms, this job is *so* hard. This motherhood ride is full of the sharpest turns and steepest hills but it changes about as fast a rollercoaster too. Just like a rollercoaster has a lot of twists and turns that you love and hate and hold your breath for, for rollercoaster junkies, it all just mixes together for the wildest, best ride of your life that you would line up for all over again as soon as it is done. This is motherhood. This is the lack of personal space. This is the stretching and growing that happens in the middle of it all.

8.

Supper and Bedtime: The Two Fiercest Battlegrounds of Motherhood

"What's for supper?"

I don't know about you, but this question evokes a strong feeling inside of me. Feeding kids in general. If you have ever had toddlers, you have likely been privileged to the experience of giving your child exactly what they asked for—and they fall on the floor crying.

I am not sure what it is about food and toddlers, but I think it is possibly their way of exercising this new skill of choice and opinion that they are honing. They like to hone it over and over when it comes to food. Whether it is crusts on and they wanted them off, or they wanted half off and half on, or they wanted the jam in the shape of a smiley face, or you just literally served it on the wrong color of plate; there is so much about feeding kids that can drive parents to the edge of insanity. I have actually needed a mommy time out more than once when it comes to food battles over the years. Do not be afraid to step out of the situation for a moment if you must. Nothing can make you feel more insane or unappreciated than the battle over food.

The food your kids will eat today, will not necessarily carry over to tomorrow. They will latch onto one or two, maybe three things that lack any serious nutritional content and they will make those their staples for the next year and a half. These are the years where you are sure that your child will have scurvy from lack of vegetables and you will feed them something you never dreamed of, every day for over a year, simply to get something, anything, into that little body. How they are blasting through clothing sizes at Mach 2 is beyond you. It is okay. This season will pass, and in not too long they will be eating you out of house and home and your bank account will be longing for the days that they lived off fishy crackers, apple sauce, garlic sausage, and plain bread slices.

Just tonight, I opened Facebook and the first post was a parent lamenting suppertime and will this stage ever end. The results in the comments were definitely divided! Some say yes, and some say no. When I was a kid, I was feeding our dog one night and my mom overheard me saying to the dog, "I know Casey, the same thing *again*. This is how I feel about hamburger goulash every single day." My mom still laughs about it now. To be fair, we didn't actually have it every single night, it just felt like it to me. I turned out to love food (except hamburger goulash) and I am not picky at all anymore. So, I guess there is hope. But for now, the supper hour does not bring me a lot of joy.

I have heard the hour before dinner called "the arsenic hour" by a friend, and it is rather fitting. That hour before dinner where everyone goes from pleasant to crying. They are all hurting each other. Everyone wants a snack, even though you said no at least once a minute for the last hour. To which they fall on the floor like their skeleton just turned to Jell-o and they insist they are so hungry they might die and their legs no longer work. Bearing in mind they had a snack about an hour ago. You mutter something about children that actually are starving who would love this cooking, and you step over them while making supper. I find myself saying "good, if you are that hungry, then you might actually eat your supper without complaining tonight." To which they reply, "Well what *is* for supper?" followed by, "*I hate that*!!!". Every single night.

Once in awhile, you win the lottery and everyone devours their dinner. You make a mental note of what it was and that you will be making that again soon. Next time you make it, they hate it and will not touch it. The more kids you have, the more they tend to play off each other as well. Something that one kid used to love, now he or she hates it because a sibling was acting like you were trying to poison them with their dinner. I find myself feeling burned out at the very idea of making dinner because there are so few wins that make everyone, or anyone under the age of seven, happy. Have you ever been sitting at the dinner table, or making dinner, and the kids announce that they do not like what is for supper and you hear yourself say, "I just don't actually care."? I feel weary at the idea of fighting the meal battles for another day. On one hand, I try to make food that everyone likes, because I don't want to fight about it again. On the other hand, I want them to learn that they might actually like something if they try it.

Parents everywhere manage this in many ways. Like everything, there is not a right or a wrong way to go about the dinner battle. Some people will spoon-feed their kids for years. Some will make them stay at the table for hours until they eat. Some will give their kid the food from last night in the morning so they learn that they need to finish their plate. Just like everything with kids, the success of all these methods varies to the same degree as kids and their personalities vary. Personally, the only thing I really stick to, is to really try to not have food battles at other people's homes. I know that whatever battle I pick, I need to stick with it. I do not want to do this at someone else's home. I try and pick carefully what I think my kids will eat and I tell them, "We do not say we don't like something at someone else's table. You are polite and will not be rude with your words or actions." We win some. We lose some. Like when my child makes a fake gagging sound at someone else's table.

Thus far, I have not found a magic answer to this battle. Be kind to yourself for the fact that maybe you don't cook as many delicious things as you used to; that your repertoire has dwindled to a bunch of safe meals, including breakfast for dinner every week. Whatever it takes for all of you to get to the table and share time and space together in a way that is good for your family, do it. This is the time where you have the opportunity to connect in a way that is not as distracted (aside from the twenty times you get up from the table to get something, even though you have asked multiple times if anyone needs anything else), and actually talk to each other. However it looks to get a meal together that may not be a fight, remind yourself that you are still awesome, even if it is not what you wish you were making, or is the same thing you had three days in a row. For all the days that an enjoyable meal experience feels like a pipe dream, tomorrow is always a new day. Maybe the best you can hope for is to just think to yourself that you are going to be grateful for the fact that you have this family that you get to feed.

Now you have made it through suppertime and it is bedtime. I used to dream about bedtime being this idyllic time where we snuggle and read books and give hugs and kisses and say good night. Everyone feels loved. With our first child, we actually had a pretty great routine for a long time. He loved his crib, so we kept him there as long as we could. Then he stayed in his little toddler bed as if it was a crib. Until one day he didn't. That was the day that bedtime went downhill. You have these high hopes that everyone will drift off to sleep with happy feelings that the last thing they heard was "Good night, I love you." Then one day, your child, who will never drink a glass of water without a fight all day long, needs six drinks before he or she can go to sleep. This inevitably leads to the child needing to pee. And of course, the need to poop comes on strong as soon as you say good night. Every ache, pain, and hangnail hurts more than it ever hurt before, as soon as the lights are out.

All the philosophical, deep questions about life must be answered. You start off kind, and hurry them back into their beds. Another hug, another kiss. I love you, good night. But it keeps going, they keep coming out. You set an early bedtime for both their wellbeing and your sanity. Now they are cutting into your time after they go to bed. It is a mental struggle as to whether we go to bed as soon as they do, or we stay up and get something done in peace, or spend time with our spouse and actually finish a conversation together—and now they are carving into that precious time. Slowly, the frustration starts to well up when they are calling, "Mom" from the top of the stairs or the end of the hall for the tenth time. You don't even go see them this time, you finally yell, "Just go to sleep!!" and you hear this little scurrying back to their bed, and the sound of quiet cries from their room. Now you feel guilty, because this is not how you wanted this to go. You do not want your kids to go to sleep to the sound of your mad voice. This happens to the best of us. You are not alone. Many times, it has resulted in both of our tears, in my kids whimpering that I yelled at them, me having to say sorry, and also pleading with them to just go to sleep rather than get up so many times that I get frustrated.

Then, the most amazing thing happens. They fall asleep. You have survived another day. Another suppertime. Another bedtime. Now, this sweet little love that does hold your heart is fast asleep, and you go in and stand there staring at them with your heart bursting out of your chest because you love them in a way you never ever imagined. Leaning in, a little kiss, a quiet "I love you," and all the strength and courage for a new day tomorrow. This is motherhood.

9.

"I Will Never Let My Kids Do That"

Remember the days that you were the perfect parent? Before kids, when you said, "I said I would never do that." We all had ideals of how we were going to manage our kids, and suddenly, when faced with the exact situation that you had watched play out before your eyes pre-kids, you stare it down, and maybe with absolute conscious awareness, or maybe the realization comes later, you do exactly what you said you would never do. Don't worry, we have *all* been there. And if you haven't been there yet, you will. This is where we heap extraordinary amounts of grace on ourselves.

I remember a time with vivid clarity when I had two kids, a one and two-year-old, I was pregnant with our third, and I was likely sick, tired, grumpy, and desperate for them to entertain themselves. I had given them a bowl of popcorn in the living room, which quickly turned into absolute mayhem. They had dinosaurs that were chomping mouthfuls of popcorn and it was everywhere. But they were playing. I had this bright idea that if we contained it, it would be tidier and they would play longer. So, I brought in the kiddie pool, blew it up, and filled it with bowls and bowls full of popcorn. Right in the living room. I threw in a whole bunch of toys and let them go to town in there. It was a disaster and I am pretty sure I cleaned up popcorn for weeks and maybe even months. But in that moment, that was the choice I made.

I find myself often doing a quick risk assessment of how bad this could turn out. Limb risk? Life risk? No? Okay, seems safe enough. Perhaps my background as an emergency room nurse plays into this quick assessment but I have, at times, walked past the stairs where the kids have all the couch cushions piled up and they are leaping through the air and landing on the pile of pillows—and I did not say a word. Again, perhaps not something I would have condoned as a good idea before kids. I probably would have gone home and told my husband about it with some judgment and horror. Yet, now I tell myself they will remember these activities for the rest of their lives and chalk it up to memory making, which makes me feel much better about it.

It does not take long as you dive into the throes of motherhood and exhaustion that you start doing what it takes to survive. To change the from ideals to facing the reality. Sometimes, it is not an easy transition. There will be moments where you just do it and give it thought later, but many times this will bring about a wrestling within your spirit. Is this okay? I said never. I judged others for this very thing. But I have to, in order to survive this moment, this hour, this day. Maybe you are new to motherhood and this is the first time you have wrestled with this, or maybe you are a seasoned veteran, but these moments are still coming up for you. Let me tell you this: It is okay. Grace for yourself. More grace for others in situations that you judged before. Commit to being better from this day forward, less judging, more supporting. Less judgment, more grace. Less judgment, more understanding that there are always layers we do not see. Do this for others, and do this for yourself. You are your hardest critic as a parent. Grace heaped upon grace.

To be totally honest, sometimes those split-second decisions will work out and you will be grateful for the choice you made in that moment. Other times however, they will not work out. They will come back to bite you. It will happen. It just does. Learn from it. Course correct. Apologize or remediate the situation if it calls for it. Move on.

Have you ever had your partner ask you for an opinion? You do a quick mental check and throw out a simple "Whatever you think is best, it doesn't matter to me." You go about your business and they go about theirs, and they come back and ask you to come check out the project. You stand there for a brief moment trying to mask any thoughts on your face while you look at a situation and realize, "I never dreamed it would turn out this way and it turns out I do, in fact, have an opinion on that." However, you already played your hand. You already said it didn't matter to you. So, you quickly and nicely smile and say, "It's great. Thank you." Maybe you are not that gracious in the moment. It has taken me awhile to get to the place where I recognize my own part in how that turned out by saying I didn't have an opinion so now I need to be grateful for how things are, and the work my husband did. I find many of my decisions as a mom are often like this too. I do a quick assessment of all of our needs in that moment and make a choice. Sometimes I am very proud of myself, and other times I think, "Wow, I did not anticipate that they would take it that far and that they would do *that* in this situation."

There will be times where you have to laugh or you will cry for hours when you realize how far down the rabbit hole everyone is, and you might as well let this play out while they are still busy and deal with the aftermath later. These are the times where you remind yourself again that this is what memories are made of. They will always remember the day that Mom told them they could turn on the hose for a minute outside to get a little drink of water, and the next time you looked outside there was a mud pit half way to Japan and you can't see anything but the whites of your child's eyes and you are completely horrified by the whole scene, but all you hear are shrieks of delight and the pure joy. It's okay. You can hose them off outside. Carry them right to the tub. Clothes can be washed; tubs can be cleaned. Your ability to hold it together and let them have fun will be what they remember. This might be a stretch for some of us, but what if you even joined them? You let yourself get super muddy and you joined in the fun and pretended that you were a kid again. You got in there, laughed and got messy with them. Sometimes our ability to surprise our kids with this kind of spontaneity is just what we all need to just take a deep breath and savour the moments with them.

Raising kids is hard. We need to make so many choices and decisions about them and for them, in order to keep them alive and thriving. We are faced with saying no a lot of the time and we can get bogged down in this. Sometimes just saying yes and putting aside all the other things for a little while can be the most freeing thing you do for yourself. Some of my favourite moments as a mom are when I stop with the to-do list and deep dive into something that makes my kids eyes go wide in amazement that mom did that with them. I get silly, messy, and crazy and see the sparkle in their eyes at the sheer delight of it all. These are also the same memories that we *also* remember for the rest of our lives.

10.

Travelling with Kids

Travelling with kids. Do you do it? Have you done it? Do you love it? Would you rather poke yourself in the eye or crawl across hot coals? There are so many factors that come into play when you think about travelling with kids. To be honest, we did not do it much when our first and even second were really small. My oldest child hated his car seat. Any parents out there feel me as soon as I say that? Maybe they scream all the time and you basically never leave the house unless it is absolutely necessary. Hats off to you, do not let a single person judge you for your choice. Until they have ridden a mile in your car, people do not have any right to tell you what it is that you need to be doing with your life.

Being in a car with a screaming child is something akin to torture. I have heard of parents buying multiple new car seats just on the hopes that they will find something that makes this sweet little pterodactyl comfortable enough to stop screaming. Then there is the child who is fine as long as the vehicle is moving. However, nothing speeds up the heart rate and gets the blood pressure rising more than the sight of a light turning yellow as you approach it, and you cannot possibly speed up enough to blast through it and spare yourself the risk of this sweet little human starting to scream.

Alas, you have to stop sometimes and it goes from peaceful, to the first squeaks, to full on crying in what feels like a matter of seconds. If you are in the passenger seat, you are suddenly trying to contort your body and stretch your arms in ways they were never meant to bend, just to simply locate that soother in the rear facing car seat and hopefully jam it in your baby's mouth without accidentally sticking it in their eye, causing all the "mom fail" emotions and a screaming child that isn't going to stop crying now, even though the light changed to green. The icing on the cake is, if you have toddlers as well, now they are covering their ears screaming, "It's too loud in here!" and when it does not stop, they start crying too and mayhem ensues from there.

Friends, if this is you, the idea of travelling is probably not even on your radar. You may even be taking a pass on those family get-togethers for the foreseeable future, using this as a great excuse to make your own traditions anyway now that you have kids. Do not let other people make you feel bad about your choices. Those times in the car are hard. Short term, you may be able to manage but if this is your normal and you know that they are going to scream for hours on end, this is not good for your sanity or your baby. It is okay to decide that this is not a season of travel for you.

I am not sure what got into us after a season of not really travelling at all with our kids when we only had two. Our oldest was that kid that cried at the lights but our second child seemed to tolerate his seat fairly well. However, I found all the paraphernalia that comes with them felt like a lot. The baby is about ten pounds' worth of space. But they come with a suitcase with no less than ten changes of clothes per day, another suitcase of diapers, a playpen, bouncy chair, a bunch of toys, bibs, blankets, and so on. It is not easy to just pack up and head out for a weekend away. You are working around naps, feeds, snacks, bed times, and moods. The concept of travel can be a daunting one. But for some strange reason, once we added a third to the mix, we suddenly got this bright idea that we should take a trip with all of them. I honestly do not know what gave me the courage to actually do it. Perhaps the fact that in my very core, travelling is part of who I am and I was craving a trip. That may have been the catalyst to the whole big adventure. So, we decided to book a trip, on a plane, with three small children.

I look back at pictures and laugh. How did we manage it? How did we pull it all off, I honestly have no idea! However, we still remember that trip with so many amazing memories. I know there was lots of hard moments. Yet, our oldest was only four and he still talks about going to California. We saw some great things and made some awesome memories and you know what I came away with? The belief in myself that we could do things like this. That we could take trips, even though in this season it is a total crapshoot if the good is going to outweigh the bad and if we would feel like it was worth it when we got home. It also gave me the belief in us, that we could take the risk, make the memories and do some hard things.

Sometimes, you are standing on the edge of taking the opportunity and you cannot see how it is going to work out. You can't see how it going to be successful and you just say no. I have yet to take a trip yet where I actually think to myself that I wouldn't do that again. I often say, when you have babies and toddlers, any time you go anywhere there is a seesaw where "worth it" is on one side and "not worth it" is on the other side. The "not worth it" side is tipped significantly in that side's favour a lot of the time. But then little things bring you closer to balance while you are gone, and thankfully, our brains tend to remember the good easier than the bad. By the time we are home, even if you pile all the good and all the hard together on the seesaw, it might be heavily weighted in the "too hard" favour, yet, all the times we came back to balance on the trip make us feel like we want to do it again. Over time, the balance happens more often. It gets easier. You spent more time on the "worth it" side of the seesaw.

However, often as soon as you feel like you have arrived in the travel game, someone hits a new stage and different things tip the scales to the hard side. Kids are like that. They want to keep us on our toes. On our last big trip, it was not our littlest that made it harder, it was the stage our oldest was in. He was easily frustrated by not getting what he wanted and he felt like we were not doing enough for him. I found myself struggling not to be angry at him. Not to grab him by the shoulders and look him in the eye and tell him how much we were spending to give him a trip and these memories and he should be grateful. Honestly, I felt a bit defeated. I felt like we should be at a place where vacations are full of so much fun and this should be easy. Then I remembered that we are taking them out of routine, food choices are not great, there are late nights and early mornings. It is a balance to remember that they are not always going to be their best, and neither am I. But the beauty of being together for a trip is that we are typically more engaged and have more opportunity for conversation, some amazing lasting memories, and more time together actually getting along. Watching our kids have these new experiences where they play, imagine, and are filled with wonder *together* feels magical. At home, we can get into those cycles where they are always fighting with each other. Often, travel allows them to be friends with each other. Until they have been pent up in car for too long together, and then all bets are off. Hopefully a stop, a hotel pool, and a swim are in your near future at that point.

When we were buying a new minivan (if you aren't team minivan, I won't judge you but I'm just going to say that sliding doors are a gift to parents and this is simply the easiest, most kid-friendly vehicle on earth and holds the most remarkable amount of stuff in the back, plus mine has a vacuum in the back), we went into the dealership and the salesman asked us what our top three things were that we were looking for in a van. Being the safety-conscious, child-focused mom that I am, I said, "Sirius radio, heated seats, and DVD players in the back for long trips."

The salesman said, "Okay, we also have lots of safety features including cabin watch where you can turn on this video camera in the back, and you can actually watch your kids and see what they are doing."

To which I replied, "That's great, but do you have any vans where there is privacy glass like a limo that comes up at the push of a button, and it blocks out all the sound and noise and we could call it cabin don't watch? Do you have anything like that?"

He looked at me with some serious uncertainty in his eyes, and my husband chimed in and said, "Do you have kids?" He said he did not, so my husband just said "you'll understand one day." Then we laughed and he knew we were joking. Sort of.

To this day, there is a little symbol on our dash that does nothing, but when our kids are driving us crazy in the back, we pretend to push it for the privacy glass and oddly, it makes us laugh and feel just a tiny bit better.

Vehicle rides with kids is not easy. We already talked about what it is like to ride in the car with a screaming baby. That is next-level hard. However, there is also a certain level of intensity of riding with kids of any age. Do you have any talkers in your family? We have a couple. I remember recently, my husband picked up our son after a day camp and they had to run a couple of errands before they got home, and they came in and our son was still chattering and asking questions. Finally, my husband gave me this wide-eyed look and said, "Someone is a question factory today and I need a little mental break."

As a child, I remember thinking about how lucky my dad was that I did not really sleep in the car. I would stay awake and talk to him. Looking back now I can only imagine how many times he thought to himself, I wish she would go to sleep or *just stop talking* to me. That ghetto blaster with headphones was probably one of my parent's favourite purchases. Yet, I have no memories of him ever being anything but patient when he listened to me talk and answered my questions. I hope my own kids feel like that about me when they look back. However, I can say with total transparency, I have asked everyone to stop talking to me at certain points because I think my brain is going to explode from the input. There is something amazing about the conversation with kids in the car. At the same time, there is also something very amazing about a few minutes of silence too.

Have you ever left on a road trip and it is going to be hours in the car, only to have someone asking how long until we are there before you hit the first stop sign at the end of your street? The kids are already fighting in the back seat and someone managed to poke someone else in the eye. There are tears. And you just left the house. You have probably spent days getting ready for this trip. Planning, packing, prepping, and bringing all the snacks. Everyone is set up with their water bottle, their best stuffed animal and their blanket, no one is wanting for a thing, and yet, there they are asking how long until we are there, they are fighting with siblings, and you wonder why you bothered with all of this.

It can be tricky to wrestle your way through these emotions. If the truth be told, it is often not gracious or loving when I turn around and respond to these things. It basically comes out in a loud voice where I declare how hard I worked for this trip and now all they are doing is fighting and complaining and would everyone rather go home? Not my best self. Not a shining example of grace. I often need to apologize. At times I am reminded that how do I expect them to show up differently when I am showing up this way? It is not perfect but I am trying to stop and take a deep breath. It is okay to be firm but still not answer in anger, and to set the tone for our family trip as one of respect for each other. The ability to travel as a family is actually a gift. The opportunity to make memories with the kids that they will remember for a lifetime is my delight and joy. It is a privilege and I need to spend a little more time thinking of it that way. But in those trenches leading up to the trip—kids cannot wear their favourite clothes because you need to wash and pack them, which results in so many tears for what feels unnecessary, the late nights, the balance of working together with your partner to get ready, which likely results in one or more tense conversations (or maybe that's just me?), the prepping snacks and drinks, ensuring you have diapers, blankets, toys, activities for the car, all the things, as well as organizing pets—it is not easy. It can be hard to take a deep breath when the trip does not get off on the right foot.

Take a deep breath if you need to. Say sorry if you say something you shouldn't, or if you yell. Refocus. This is going to be fun. You will make memories. I promise. It is kind of like childbirth. You don't forget all of it. But just enough to do it again when the opportunity arises. My kids ask to live in a hotel. I find hotel life is kind of like mayhem where kids don't sleep the best, they stay up too late, and we are all crammed together in one space, but the look in their eyes when we are going to a hotel is sheer delight. It is worth it.

11.

The Re-Entry Phase

The re-entry phase is a real thing. I came up with the term re-entry phase after having been away with my husband for a night when our kids were young. However, in talking with many other moms, this seems to be a real phenomenon with kids. There can be multiple different reasons for the re-entry phase, but ultimately it is the process of readjusting to regular routine with all the people that live under one roof coming back together at home.

When I first noticed the re-entry phase, we had come home from a night away from our two boys, who were one and almost three at the time. We got a glowing report of good behaviour and kindness toward each other, with good manners and good listening. All was well. Grandma and Grandpa stayed for a little while and then headed home for some much-needed rest. We had not been apart from our kids much up to this point and we had missed them. We were anxious to get home to them, and excited for their squeals of delight to see us. Now we were going to sit together, snuggle, and enjoy time together since we were feeling refreshed after a night away.

Fast forward a mere half an hour or so. Kids are fighting. One just bit the other. Behaviours are escalating. Kids are not obeying. *Where* did the well-mannered kids go? Suddenly, you are wondering why the hurry to get back, looking longingly at your partner that you have not finished a sentence with since you arrived home, and the relaxed manner in which you arrived is quickly fading into a mere memory.

Have you been there? Have you felt like this? And then felt guilty for feeling this way? You are not alone. I often have to remind myself over and over that this is normal. They missed us and now they are acting out in the safety of their relationship with us as their parents, vying for attention. Have you ever seen or heard about the studies that seem to be done every couple of years that prove that kids act the worst for their moms? As a mom, do you ever hear those results and think, "Wow, that is so interesting. I never would have guessed!!" No, what you likely thought was that no one needed to do a study to prove what is already clear every day in your home.

We all know that kids act the worst for us. We are their safe space. The place where they know they are loved unconditionally. Let that sink in for a moment and feel all those warm happy feelings from that thought. Because once they start acting out in those behaviours, it can be very difficult to tap back into that warm happy space rather than also acting out in the most unbecoming ways. This is also true for the re-entry phase. They are safe when you are back with them again. In these instances, I try to be ready for it. I do not rush home, but rather savour the drive back and remind myself to be ready for it. I do my best to be very present with them. Lots of snuggles, hugs and time. I brace myself for the question of "What else did you bring me?" when I give my children their gifts that we chose for them while we were away. I do not always execute the re-entry phase well, but once acknowledged that it happens and it does not just happen to us, it has allowed me to be a bit more gracious about it and to be a bit more mentally prepared when it happens.

Another type of re-entry is when you go away with your kids and you have all been on a family holiday for a few days, or a week, or maybe even longer. There are many things that happen on these adventures. One of them is typically a lot of late nights. Another thing is that the kids often eat lots of snacks along the way and their dining choices are not always what they would be at home. Plus, you are typically doing lots of fun things and focusing on the stuff that you think the kids would love to do. Family holidays are such amazing memory makers. When I think back to my own childhood memories and holidays, I never think about what I did not get, I think about what we did and where we went and what memories we made. Chances are really high that I was not always a grateful child that loved everything we did, made it easy to travel, and did not beg for one million stuffed animals at every gift shop that we went through, and pouted when I did not get them. I mean, I love to think that I was perfect, but I suspect my parents would be very quick to shed some light on that delusion.

I do think when we are in holiday mode, we say yes more often. To the activities, the souvenirs, the treats. It is fun to say yes more often and see your kids' eyes light up when they are expecting a no and you say yes. It is amazing to watch life through their eyes as they experience new places and fun things. I don't even think we need to change that, but it is setting us up for a re-entry phase struggle when we arrive back home. My own personal opinion is that we just need to be ready for it and expect it, so it is not a shock when it happens. It will happen. We all arrive home in a state of exhaustion, dirt and stickiness, with hearts full of memories, and possibly at least one screaming child. On the last day of travel, you are often pushing hard to get home and this often involves a longer drive and less stops, and you drive a little too long or it is late, and about an hour from home, someone can't take it anymore and the tears start. Not the best endnote of a great holiday, but at least it makes you happy to arrive home.

Over the next few days as everyone readjusts back to life, the kids start to complain. They are bored and want to live in a hotel for life. They don't want to eat what you are cooking because they like the kid-friendly options of all the restaurant menus and you aren't dishing up pizza, or hamburgers and fries, or chicken strips tonight. They want treats and snacks on demand, and are still lamenting the fact that you said no to that one stuffed animal that they will miss for the rest of their life, even though they came home with three others. But that panda, in that one store that you did not go back to, that was the one that they wanted and all the others were a big letdown. You find yourself getting frustrated because you are tired too; this trip was an investment and they just keep asking for more. I know I sometimes find myself finally bursting out with something really helpful like, "Don't you know how hard we worked to have this holiday, how about a little gratitude for what you did get, and all the things you got to do, rather than sitting here complaining about the other stuff. How about that?" Which is not very helpful in these situations. Chances are, I made someone cry and I did absolutely nothing to help them actually look at what we did with gratitude at all.

We are all a work in progress here. This is another one of those awesome opportunities to help teach your kids what it looks like to apologize to each other. I have those learning opportunities pretty often. I try to stop myself from an outburst and start a reasonable conversation talking about our good memories. Maybe slowing down a little on all the things I'm trying to catch up on after being away, and just sitting with them, looking at pictures, talking about our trip, the memories, remembering that they just had most of our undivided attention for the whole holiday and that is a change for them now that we are home. There are lots of pieces to the re-entry phase and the feelings that come with it. Kids just express outwardly what we, as adults, wish we could express. Come home with grace for yourselves, patience for your kids, and the expectation of a few rough days. Set your expectations a little lower for catching up on all the things on your list. I have a lot of amazing memories of a lot of trips and holidays as a kid and I don't have a single memory of the re-entry phase, or all my unmet expectations of any of the trips.

The last re-entry phase struggle I'm going to talk about is my own. Mommas, have you ever gone away for a night, two nights, or a week, and you come home thinking you are going to be so refreshed and the most patient mom ever, but instead, you struggle? You feel this ache in your heart that you should not be struggling so much after you just had a break, and yet, you are still struggling!

I feel you. I get it. You are not alone, or a bad mom. When you go for one night, it seems like you finally just stopped hearing phantom shrieks for "*Mom*!!!" and it is already time to go back. When you go for two nights, you may have had two good sleeps and even a nap, but it is actually just enough to make you more tired before you start to feel less tired (Does anyone else feel more tired for a few days before you start to feel rested when you have the opportunity for improved sleep?), and now it is time to go back. Or maybe you just had the luxury of a week away. You had full conversations with your partner or your friends. Your hot drinks never got cold, and you had the best week of sleep you've had since becoming a mom. You did things for yourself like reading a book, taking a nap, or following through on a thought or maybe even a bunch of them. You held hands that weren't small and sticky. No one fought over who was going to sit beside mommy at every meal, and you only had to cut up your own meat. You lingered in bed in the morning without the impending sense of children bursting in at any time. Oh, and you missed your kids. For sure you did. You saw other kids doing things on your time away and you felt the ache in your heart to see your own kids doing these things too. So many things reminded you of them. You and your husband told each other stories about your kids that you had forgotten to tell each other before. You were ready to get home and hug those kids and snuggle up to hear about their time away from you and what they did, as well as tell them about the things you did and saw that made you think of them. You're pretty sure you are going to be the best mom ever once you are home. Unendingly patient.

However, about twenty minutes after you have arrived home, you have heard the word "mom" about two hundred times. Your children don't even know what they want to say, it seems they just want to say mom over and over again. They are talking over each other. The demands are fast and furious for your attention, and to get all the things, and to tell you everything that they feel matters the most, and you are a little out of practise from the onslaught of demands on your attention. Your children have officially become like the seagulls fighting over the fish in Finding Nemo, yelling "Mine! Mine! *MINE!*" and you can feel the overwhelm creeping in. Readjusting back to reality is no joke.

After a day or more to yourself, remembering what it felt like to have more brain space to think, read, carry on full conversations and be creative, felt amazing. I hope you savoured every minute of it without a hint of guilt for being away. This is a necessary break for our brains. It is so good for us to have this time. Loving every minute of it, it is not wrong and it does not make you a bad mother, and craving it as soon as you get home is normal. When you change a habit, the immediate period afterward is when you think of it, crave it, and long for it the most. Time to be you apart from your kids is kind of like this too. It is just different than the day-to-day in the trenches and those moments to think and be creative were so enjoyable, it is okay to crave them. You will to find your groove, and find joy in being back with your kids. The amazing, loving mom did not change, but having time to reconnect with yourself and your spouse or friends is precious.

So, when you're struggling with your own re-entry phase, first off, give yourself grace. Second, think gratitude. Think about how grateful you are to have had that time away, all the things that you did while you were gone, what you enjoyed, and why you are so grateful for the time. Then think about all the things in front of you that you are grateful for. Coming home to your kids, that you have kids that missed you and are craving your attention and love. Give yourself time outs if you need to. If your kids are small enough, lining laundry baskets with blankets and giving them a little pillow and lining them up like a little movie theatre is a great trick to buying yourself some time and you should get at least ten minutes of peace. Maybe they have a little extra screen time. Pour yourself a glass a wine. Whatever it takes to get you over the hump, lean into those things. The biggest thing is to not give in to the feelings of guilt that you should not feel this way, or feel like you are a bad mom for having these feelings. That time away was revitalizing and you will see the benefits, but those first days can be a bit rough.

12.

A Day in the Life of a Mom

Two days ago, I went to my daughter's dance class. She is three and she does a little ballet class with a bunch of other adorable little ballerinas. We all show up there by 9:00 a.m. with our little girls. Some moms have other smaller kids that run around while their bigger sisters dance. Moms chat. Most are moms that work out of the home. Some work shift work. Some of us managed to get our tea or coffee on the way, sometimes we have to go back out to get it because we just did not have time before the class started. We all have a story that got us to this place with our little dancers and got them all lined up and ready to head into the room.

On this particular day, I brought my daughter into the bathroom to go pee before her class and one mom was sitting on the floor, with her littler daughter having a full meltdown because she wanted the green tutu and not the pink one, but her big sister was going to wear the green one in the class. If it was in my home, chances are high that if one kid wanted something, the others would insist on needing that colour, thus creating this war between children as they stake their claim on what must be "theirs." I'm not sure what the story was in this case. I just carefully stepped around them, gave Mom a knowing smile and tried to just leave them to work out the details. Eventually they came out and the class started, and she sat on the floor and we started chatting. But she was rubbing her leg and off-handedly commented that she had fallen down the stairs that morning. No big deal. Just a fall down the stairs. Obviously, she was okay because she made it to the class, but it got me thinking about how this is motherhood in many ways.

From the moment we wake up in the morning, all the factors are at play. Moods, late bed times, poor sleeps, sick kids, disagreements with spouses, kids to get off to school, lunches to be made, breakfasts to serve, myriad other requests to fulfill, appointments to get to. Some days feel dreamy. They go off without a hitch. Kids wake up happy. They play, agree, compromise, have patience, I love you is spoken through the day, hugs and kisses are given, and it feels like a delight. A true gift. But what about those days where it is not this way? Which feels like most days. It would be rare to have a day like that for the whole day.

I find myself treading lightly in the mornings in hopes we can do our best to start the day gently and without incident. But kids don't really care about that. They just show up with all their big feelings, good or bad, and lay all the cards on the table. Some mornings are barely survived. Here is the kicker, if kids are in a bad mood, chances are good it is because they did not sleep well, which probably means Mom slept even worse. So now we are trying to navigate these human balls of big feelings and we are struggling to maintain our own composure. But how do you show up with your best self when you are beyond exhausted as well? Often, not very well. This can be such a struggle, especially in the mornings when we need to get somewhere or get kids out the door to school or to the bus, especially if we need to be ready as well.

Please bear in mind that we do not owe the world a hurricane of energy. We live in a society where full, busy schedules are expected. When people would ask me how I was doing I realized I was saying, "Good, so busy," as my opening line all the time. Personally, I don't want that to be the defining characteristic of my life, so I work on how I answer that question. In reality, even our very definitions of busy is different from family to family, and it is the individual family unit that gets to decide how that looks for their household. Do not let anyone question what you do or do not take on for yourself and your family. No one is back home in the trenches of overwhelmed children offering to give you a break if everyone is not coping with the schedule you are maintaining. Some days one child feels like the work of six. Other days three seems like a breeze. Choose your best "yeses" for your family, and be proud of the times that you say no to something that will not serve you or your family unit.

That being said, there are times when life just seems to speed up and you are holding on for dear life. Give yourself room in these seasons to do just your best. You will forget things. Your child will sadly remind you that you forgot to send his library book to school and he did not get to pick a new one that week, and that sad face will feel like a knife to your heart. Next week is a new week. He will get a new book then. Maybe you missed an activity one week because you thought it was Tuesday and it was actually Wednesday. Or suddenly it is 5:00 p.m. and you forgot to think about dinner. Order pizza. From the moment we get up as moms, we are thinking about the day. What will be for dinner, what should I take out of the freezer, who needs to be where and when, do we need groceries, when did I do the laundry last, the bathrooms are filthy, the hamster cage needed cleaning four days ago, the hot lunch orders are due today, I need to pack the swimming lesson bag early and make sure I have snacks so we can leave as soon as the kids walk in the door from school. The day ends and you feel like you did not accomplish a thing, when really you accomplished hundreds. Hundreds of tiny little details that add up to a rich life that you are building for your family. A delicate balance of maintaining a home, a career, friendships, a relationship, and kids. Meeting basic needs, and going beyond that to provide opportunities, give love and affection, and create this rich tapestry of a home full of memories that your kids will look back on. What will they remember that more than anything? That Mom loved us.

There is so much juggling behind the scenes that we do not talk about. It is *hard* in those day-to-day trenches of life. The lists of things to do, errands to run, kids to get to appoints, and activities, jobs to be at, meals to plan, all while raising humans with values, morals, attachment and love. There are days when we slip at the top of the stairs, probably on a toy someone left lying around that you already asked them to pick up; we fall down the stairs, get up and herd everyone out the door. Let us stop for a second and think about that. How amazing are *you*, as a mom, to execute life this way? It is remarkable, if you really think about what goes into a day in the life of a mom.

13.

May I Have Your Attention Please?

As I mentioned earlier, I'm not actually sure who invested money into a study to prove that kids behave the worst for their moms over anyone else. It also seems like they re-do this study here and there because I have heard of this more than once since I became a mom. I feel that the money spent on this could have been better spent on almost anything else other than running a study to show something that every mom already knows. However, I guess there is something validating to our mental health that proves to us that we are not crazy, this is a scientifically proven phenomenon that happens.

If we think about human nature, it would make sense. We all actually tend to save the worst of ourselves for the people we love the most, because they love us. They accept us as we are and they know that we are not always like this. Depending on where you are at in this motherhood journey, it might actually feel like you have not seen that best part of yourself for a while. I assure you; you are probably not giving yourself enough credit. You are exhausted and I promise that you will start to feel more normal in time. How many times though, do we put on the happy face and show up outside of our homes as this smiling, happy person? But it is all we have. By the time we get back to a place of safety, we allow our guard down. Sometimes, it is not pretty.

I don't know why, but when I walk into a room, my kids instantly start fighting when they had been playing so nicely before. How often do you hear quiet and you are scared to go look? You go through all the things that *could* be going wrong and wonder if any of it is worth the risk of disrupting the peace, the comradery of the kids actually being friends to each other. We have all been there. You have chanced it and did look, and it was *way* worse than you were expecting. You are both relieved you checked and angry at what you see in front of you.

I remember the time my boys were in the bathroom on our main floor. I was in the living room and I could tell that there was no water running. I had no idea what they were doing, but what could they be doing? No running water in a bathroom seems pretty safe. I poked my head in the door after a while and, to my horror, they had soaked roll after roll of toilet paper in the toilet water and had proceeded to throw giant wet balls of toilet paper on all the walls, floor and ceiling of my bathroom! There is also the opposite where you have also peek around the corner like a ninja and they *were* playing nicely and they happened to look up just at that moment and saw you and started fighting instantly, and you feel the disappointment and regret welling up inside of you that you ruined the moment. Then there is the rare gem of a time that you peek around the corner and they are just being friends. Maybe they see you, maybe they don't, but it does not matter, they just play. You find yourself standing there marvelling at what amazing little humans they are and this is why you had more than one, so they would have a buddy, a playmate, a friend. You stand there and you are grateful. These moments can be life sustaining on the long days.

Most Saturday mornings, my sweet husband gets up with the kids when we are having a quiet day at home or we don't have plans in the morning. I cherish these times. Sometimes I get extra sleep, lots of times I just doze and enjoy the time to have thoughts to myself because I can hear all the household noise. If my husband sleeps in, no one even bothers going in to ask him for things, but if I am in bed, the kids still need to pop in and just check if I am actually in bed sleeping, like Dad said. Or they stand right outside our bedroom door and shout at the top of their lungs downstairs that they need help. So it is hard to actually sleep, but I enjoy just listening to the bustle of the house. Oftentimes, they are happy, laughing and enjoying each other's company. I think to myself that I should get up so I can enjoy the happiness of family time. I quietly come down the stairs and they are playing or sitting at the table colouring, or maybe watching a movie all piled up on daddy on the couch. I plan to just slip into this bliss. However, they see me, and they start clamouring for my attention. Fighting over who has more space on my lap. They start asking me for things and making requests. If they hurt themselves at all since they got up, even an hour before, they start to cry about it all over again to ensure I give adequate amounts of sympathy and, within minutes, the sweet integration that I had hoped for is, instead, this mounting frustration that all was peaceful and well until I set foot in the room.

The dream of grabbing a cup of tea and tucking myself in beside my husband on the couch to just sit and watch the kids be kids in our home and just share quiet, pleasant time together never materializes. It can be hard to maintain our cool in these moments. We are truly just longing for the opportunity to just enjoy watching our family be a family in their own space. In those early days with really small babies and toddlers, those moments are about as rare as a real unicorn. As our kids grow, and I realize that I do not have to just accept this as the way it is, they are big enough to go and play, we are able to set out expectations a little bit more. That they need to occupy themselves while we just sit together. It is not perfect by any means, but don't hesitate to start to slowly set new expectations and boundaries for your kids as they grow.

I know for myself, I was in survival mode for a long time and we did lots of things just to buy ourselves a moment or two, or we were resigned to just not having that time. It took me a while to realize that I was able to slowly try to impact the culture of our home as they got older. Kids are amazing little creatures that are capable of more than I often give them credit for. Likely, it will not be without indignance and some words that are well aimed to try and cause guilt that you are choosing to sit with your spouse for a few minutes rather than serve their every need. Do not own that guilt. Relationship work is so important. Time to just sit and be is so important. These are the moments where we do a quick fill on our tanks. To give us the stamina to get through another day, another week.

Speaking of clamouring for attention, can we just talk for a second about what happens when you pick up the phone to make a call and your kids are within a hundred-metre radius of where you are? I have no idea how moms ever communicated with each other before the days of texting and messaging each other. I can literally be months behind on dentist appointments and the only barrier to me making the appointment is actually picking up the phone. I fully recognize that someone will read this and shake their heads thinking that "This is exactly what is wrong with today's society and this generation." I don't even care. I actually find myself searching for online booking now, simply so I do not have to make a phone call. What on earth happens that alerts your children to you making a phone call, the second it starts ringing?

Even if you stepped into another room! It is kind of like the same weird secret alarm I swear my kids have rigged up at the doorway of my ensuite bathroom, where as soon as I place my feet on the tile floor in that room it alerts them to start yelling, "Mom!" at the top of their lungs. Every. Single. Time.

Making a phone call is basically the same. One time, I had to call customer service. I had ordered something online three times and it was cancelled three times. This is a testament to how dedicated I am to *not* making a phone call. I tried and was rejected with my order three times before I finally called customer service. So this time I had to discuss the problem with a real person. I started the call in the kitchen, which was a rookie mistake to begin with. My kids swarmed me immediately and started asking for things. The problem is that the person on the other end of the phone is asking questions and they cannot see what is happening around you. So, you are trying to answer questions but at the same time, you are also distracted by trying to silently say no and get your kids to stop talking. Now you sound like you are under the influence of something because your responses are more delayed than they should be and you are also trying to recall what she was even asking you so that you respond in some type of intelligent way. Finally, you just make a bit of a joke about your kids (on the very minuscule chance that they can't hear the chaos that you are trying to act really nonchalant about) and how they just swarm as soon as you are on the phone. If you are lucky, you get a lady on the other end that has kids and understands. If odds are stacked against you, you have someone that does not acknowledge your comment at all and now you just feel awkward.

So, you move to your bedroom and lock yourself in there. Your children follow you crying now that you are now ignoring them and they act like they are certainly going to die of thirst, starvation, or neglect in the next ten minutes while you finish this call. You manage to barricade yourself into the bedroom, but now your angry children start pounding on the door and are screaming, "Mommy!" at the top of their lungs. You move as far away from the door as possible, maybe even hiding in the closet just so you can even hear this person on the other line. A quick glance over at the door: You can see small fingers trying to reach under the door in the most pitiful way as the kids cry for you like you have left them alone for hours. This is both heart-breaking and annoying all at the same time. You finally finish your distracted customer service call, thanking them for their patience. You open the door to your bedroom and your sweaty, sobbing children lunge into your arms with tear-stained faces and inform you that they "*needed* you and you weren't there and why did you lock us out of this room?" You sit at the doorway to the bedroom holding them in your arms, making a solemn promise to yourself to try four or five times next time before you endure another phone call. With a sigh, you herd your children back to the kitchen to provide them with the snack and drink they were in desperate pursuit of, thinking about the days you thought this job was going to be easy.

I often consider that the bond we form with our kids for those nine months in utero, and then the love like no other that we are overcome with when they are born, is purely a God-given gift so that we do not follow through on the threats of selling our children. That unconditional love is sometimes all we have to get by. Those long days where we get the worst of their behaviour, and there does not seem to be enough connection, discipline, or consequences to make them want to turn it around. Some days prayer, essential oils, lots of deep breathing, and locking myself in the bathroom are the only things that get me through the day. These are the days that it is the hardest to be grateful for anything, but are also the days where we have to dig so deep to find those moments of gratitude. It might just be that you did not yell in the last ten minutes. Start with the tiniest mustard seeds of gratitude.

As moms we want to be their safe place, that haven where they come and they are loved. Yet, we get some of their worst behaviours and attitudes. It is hard to remember that this is actually part of the package, and because they love us the very best, and they feel the safest with us. Take a deep breath and in those moments where you literally can not find something to be grateful for, when you are drowning in frustration and feeling overwhelmed by their attitudes, demands, needs, clinginess, and all the poor behaviours you did not need a study to tell you about, remember that being their mom is a gift. They are not expressing it well right now, but you *are* their safe place. Know you are not alone in your feelings and you might not even like them right now. It is okay. You still love them, and the incongruence of your feelings is just part of the job. Tonight, while they are sleeping, make sure you go peek in and stare at them. These are the moments where mom hearts realign the like and love part of their feeling. In the quiet stillness of soft breaths, and peaceful faces.

14.

Sometimes You Laugh So You Don't Cry

I imagine you read that chapter title and instantly had your own story that fits into this category. As moms, we have all been there. There are so many different ways that this unfolds. Coming into a room that has been quiet for too long. Racing to find out what the crash sound was. Something that came out of your sweet child's mouth that stops you in your tracks. Those moments of sheer horror at the embarrassment that they are subjecting you to. Oh, the stories we could tell! To be honest, I kind of wish we could have a night where we all gather together with delicious food and drink and sit for hours recalling these stories. Laughing until we cry. Crying over the ones that still hurt. Joining in the comradery that is motherhood. These moments and experiences shape our motherhood story. They also make us stronger, more resilient, and often extremely creative to find remedies for the endless situations we never anticipated before we had kids.

Right from very early on, when they are just tiny little babies, there can be moments where you are totally mortified by a situation that was just a baby being a baby, but as this child's mother, it seems so much worse. I remember being at someone's house that I did not know very well, but they had known my husband for most of his life. The husband was a little hesitant to hold the baby but I assured him that he rarely even spit up. He had my son in his lap for about three minutes when my son promptly spit up right into the crotch of the man's pants. I'm sure my eyes just got huge and I start saying, "Oh my goodness, I'm so sorry!" The man looked mildly disgusted, handed me the baby and went to change. He never held another one of my children ever again.

Having a good sense of humour is essential to motherhood. It can be hard but lifesaving at the same time. Much like being a nurse, and particularly an emergency room nurse. If you did not have a slightly warped sense of humor, you might not survive. I think it is a gift that happens when you are overtired. You start to see things as funny that maybe would not otherwise be. Lean into those moments. Let them sustain you. Let them carry you through. If nothing else, they make for great stories later.

For years I said to patients in the emergency room, "How many drinks did it take to make this a good idea?" For anyone wondering, that number is variable. Then I became a mom and realized that I was going to be saying a variation of that for my whole life. "What on earth made this seem like a good idea?" "Why are you standing up there?" "Do *not* jump off that or you might die." "No, no, *NO*... do *not* pee there... too late!" "Why is that in the house? Do bugs live in the house? No? Okay, then get that thing out of here!" and on it goes.

I do not have teenagers, but I have seen enough things to know that these incidents often just end up with bigger risks and potential consequences in the teen years. So, there is that to look forward to for those of us still drowning in the impulsive toddler and young child years. Moms of teens, bless you. You have earned every single grey hair that you have either coloured or plucked, or maybe that you are embracing with grace and ease. They are a badge of honour my friends, and you wear them with pride, that you are a survivor.

I had two boys before I had a girl. My two boys are actually pretty cautious in comparison to many boys. Then I got a wild, crazy, messy little girl. My second boy loves to tidy his room and "set up" his bed. When I finally cleared out the last of the baby stuff in my daughter's room a few months ago and worked to make a space that she would think was special and she would love to play in, she walked in and looked at me and said, "Well, I like it messy better." I should have known. She is my kid who, if you give her a spoon for her soup, she will still try and eat it with the other hand instead of using the spoon.

Both my boys stayed in their cribs until we moved them out; they never tried to climb out. They kept their diapers and pajamas on every night, and for naps. We knew we had it pretty good. One Sunday when my daughter was probably about sixteen months old, I put her down for a nap. We were going to our friend's home after her nap. My husband had taken our oldest out to run a couple of errands and he was not home and we needed to leave soon, so I sent him a text to remind him that we needed to leave in about twenty minutes. I had not heard a peep on the baby monitor, so I went upstairs to gently wake up sleeping beauty and have a little cuddle before we were out the door. The smell hit me about halfway up the stairs. The lingering smell of poop. I was definitely curious about why that might be so strong. I opened the door and the smell hit me hard! I flicked on the light and there was the cutest little face looking up at me, covered in poop. When I say covered, I mean absolutely covered. Her face and hair included. I gasped. She looked at me with big eyes and held up a strand of her hair and said, "Pretty? *Pretty?*" Not really what I was thinking. It was literally everywhere she could reach, including in every little ridge and notch of the scalloped slats of her crib.

I started laughing this weird nervous laugh, quickly snapped a picture, and sent it to my husband and said, "Maybe don't hurry, doesn't look like we are going anywhere in the next fifteen minutes." I ran the bath, held her out at arm's length, and dropped her into the warm bath water. I knew I needed to get the obvious layers off her and change the water before I could hand her off to my husband to bathe, or he wasn't going to be able to handle it. Bless him, he came upstairs gagging but said he was there to help. My four-year-old ran in armed with a spray bottle of cleaner, shouting, "You shouldn't do this alone, Mom!!" and we went to work to get her, and the room, cleaned up. She stunk for days. The crib was a nightmare to clean. I can still feel my reaction right to my core of walking into that room that day. I could have cried, but thankfully this weird awkward laugh came out instead. Payback will be the photos I have saved for a rainy day in the future.

Until you are a parent, you have no idea what your parents sacrificed and did for you. It is truly remarkable what it takes to get these human beings through the early years and out into the adult world as functional members of society. This is a task we *must* take great pride in for our ability to adapt and cope and do hard things. Things we never dreamed of. The words that come out of our mouths as parents never cease to surprise even me as I say them sometimes. Things like, "Don't pee on your brother." Or, "We do not eat food in the squatting position on the table at this house." I remember when my oldest was potty training, and he loved to pee outside. We pulled into our driveway and it was very urgent that he needed to pee and he asked if he could pee outside. I told him, "Yes, but go in the back yard where it is more private." He took off running out of the garage toward the direction of the back gate. I came out around the corner in the direction he was headed and there he was with his pants around his ankles, facing the entire neighbourhood, peeing. I recall just closing my eyes and gently hanging my head, saying a quick prayer of thankfulness that we have some pretty awesome neighbors, but thinking, "Rookie mistake, you should have foreseen that and spared the neighborhood the show and told him to go inside."

The thing is, we cannot ever full anticipate what they are going to say or do. We can have some idea, but kids have a way of taking what we think might happen, and then magnifying that tenfold. It is a remarkable and amazing thing. I literally start nervous-laughing just at the very thought of how many times I have seen a situation, got a quick read and either tried to abort what I could see was about to happen, or totally just missed the cues all together, and ended up hoping and praying for grace from those who were part of the situation.

One day this past summer we were travelling. It had been a long day, and we were hitting the hot springs as our last stop. We were splitting up to get changed, girls one way, boys the other. (Full disclaimer, if any man happens to be reading this book, you might want to skip this part of the story.) I was at the start of my period and I knew I would need to hit up the bathroom before I got changed. I typically try to avoid having kids with me in the stall because they are too aware and I know questions will come. But there we were, just the two of us, and the change room was very busy. I couldn't get around taking my very chatty daughter in with me. I got her all changed and ready to go into the hot springs, and then I brought my suit to the bathroom stall and tried to ninja through this situation as quickly as possible.

By the grace of God, someone started using the hand dryer for their hair just as this moment started to unfold for me, making it slightly harder to hear for the many people sharing the change room with us. My daughter spied what was happening and started loudly shouting, "*What? What is happening? This is so gross! You are bleeding out of your bum and it is so gross. And it is so disgusting! Gross! I never want to see this ever again*!!" Then she plugged her nose and started yelling again all of the same things. I started nervously laughing involuntarily, and I was trying to get her to be quiet. I was pleading with her to stop talking, to be quiet, to just *please stop*. I quickly finished and started getting my bathing suit on. I had it halfway up when my daughter started unlocking the door and I was about to be fully on display in the mirror across from the stalls for all to see. I hissed at her to *stop* opening the door, and she turned to me and said at the top of her lungs, "*Why? So no one sees your boobs!?*" Yes, exactly. This entire situation has been so fun, that I would love to just keep my boobs to myself tonight.

To this day, I cannot think about that situation without starting to laugh nervously and feel all the feelings of that moment come flooding back. About three weeks after this happened to me, I read a story on social media about another mom's situation that was a similar experience to mine. I laughed until I cried, because I could relate. Then I read the comments and it is clear that so many of us have had these experiences, and somehow when you share them with each other, it makes it seem funnier and less humiliating. So, sweet moms, when you are in a stall experiencing your own horrifying period story involving your kids, please remember that many of us have been there. One day you will laugh a real genuine laugh about this, rather than a nervous, horrified laugh that is keeping you from bursting into tears. It is a God-given safety mechanism built into us to help us survive. Bless you friend.

15.

Mom Guilt

One night, I was chatting with a friend about the concept of this book and why I was writing it. We were chatting about how mom life is hard and we often don't really talk about it. Sure, we chit-chat here and there about different aspects and sometimes you might be very real with a couple of close friends, but right from the start I was amazed at how many things about motherhood just blew me away. Things I just didn't know. Long, hard days in the trenches. The way we constantly feel at war within ourselves. We feel like our kids will never be independent, then we lament how big they are getting ask them to stop growing. How we need a break and then we miss them like crazy when we get it. I wanted to bring it into the light, to share our stories, to start the conversation that we are all in this together. Culture, race, socioeconomic status, at the end of the day, we are all just moms that want the best for our kids. We fight for them, love them fiercely and would lay down our lives for them in a heart beat. Striving to do the best for them based on what we know, what we can do, our values and the capacity we have. It looks different for everyone, but the motivating love in our hearts for our children is the same.

As we chatted about this and how important this message is, my friend said to me, "You know, the thing I wasn't prepared for is the mom guilt." How long did it take before you realized that mom guilt is a real thing? The moment we find out that we are pregnant, we already feel some mom guilt. We do a mental recall of everything we have consumed and done in the time frame since that baby was conceived, and panic that we may have already screwed him or her up. Maybe your delivery did not go the way you planned and you already feel guilty simply for the way your baby entered the world. Or maybe you are struggling to get your milk supply in and it is not going well and you have to supplement with formula, and you feel like a failure because you were always going to be a breast-milk-only mom. On it goes. It is like moms are somehow are wired to go to the guilty side rather that to think about all the ways that we have done the right thing for that baby. How we carried him or her safely to delivery time, the hardcore way we laboured in effort to bring this human earthside, how hard we fought to keep that baby safe from the moment we knew he or she was growing inside us. When you need to supplement with formula for a short time or maybe always, rather than guilt, what if you saw yourself as the warrior that probably hand-expressed over and over when you felt bruised and in agony just to squeeze out a few drops of liquid gold, the way you fought to get your baby to latch when your nipples were cracked and bleeding and it was excruciating, but you kept fighting and cried your way through it while your baby also screamed in your arms and a stranger helped maneuver your breast into your baby's mouth in order to find the right fit for the two of you?

What if every time we fell into the mom guilt trap, we worked our hardest to think, "What am I doing right?" I know this sometimes feels impossible because it is often in our most vulnerable moments where that guilt washes over us and it can be hard to look for the other side. However, there is actually no room for mom guilt here. It will always creep back in because it is a part of mom life. I am sure there is not a mom on the entire planet that hasn't felt guilt and doesn't struggle with it on the daily, but it is lies we tell ourselves. Mom guilt is a lie. I am here to stand on the mountain tops with a megaphone and shout as loudly as I can for every single mom out there, that mom guilt is 100 percent a lie! We fall for it hook, line, and sinker over and over, but it never serves us well.

I'm not saying that this is to give us all license to behave poorly and just not feel guilty about it, obviously, but what if we gave ourselves grace? Legit, full-blown grace. To ourselves. I mentioned this definition of grace from the Cambridge Dictionary at the beginning of the book as it being "The charming quality of being polite and pleasant, or a willingness to be fair and to forgive." What if we treated ourselves this way? As well as other moms. We all do it. We are so hard on ourselves, and we are also hard on other moms. Even if we do not say something to them, we judge when someone does something different than us. But what if we had the charming quality of being polite and pleasant and were willing to be fair to ourselves and others and forgive both ourselves and others freely and willingly? Imagine if we operated from this place of value on ourselves as moms? It would be life-changing.

I wasn't going to yell, ever. Yelling hurts my heart and does not make me feel love. Why would I ever do that to my kids? I just wouldn't. Then I became a mom. I am exhausted much of the time. I operate on far less sleep that I ever thought possible on a regular basis. Lots of days I feel over-touched, over-stimulated and pulled in at least three, if not dozens of directions at one time. I often feel like I speak and no one listens. One meme that resonated with me said "I should have talked to rocks to prepare for motherhood, they listen about the same." I feel this on a deep level some days. Sometimes this comes out in me raising my voice. Every single time it happens, I cringe inside because I hate that feeling.

Sometimes outbursts happen, even though we are always striving to be better and more controlled in our responses. It happens to the best of us. You know what it does, it gives opportunity for forgiveness and discussion. Sometimes we have to apologize and it is good for our kids to know that we aren't always right either and when we aren't, we are sorry, and we mean it. This allows for opportunity for connection. Maybe you stop and get down on their level and pull them in while you are discussing what happened. Or maybe you feel like it was warranted but you have the opportunity to talk about why you are frustrated and what contributed to the interaction going in that direction. Any chance we get to reconnect and truly communicate with our kids is an opportunity well spent. But at the end of the day, let us lay aside our guilt and look for ways that we can use this opportunity to grow *with* our kids.

Just tonight I was planning to go to the movie with my littlest for a special date. I had been trying to squeeze in some work for my home business between church and going out. All three kids were supposed to be at a birthday party next door and my husband was also out running a couple of errands for me. It was quiet and I sat down to work. Ten minutes later, there was a knock at the door and my daughter was standing there crying and the neighbour kid said she had just started crying and insisted on coming home. So, I snuggled her onto the chair with a show. Then my husband started texting from the store. He does this to ensure I get what I need and to ask about things on sale. I am so grateful he does this errand for me because I hate grocery shopping. However, it just felt like every time I started something, my phone would ding again. Stop. Answer. Carry on. Then my daughter wanted a snack and then a drink. The interruptions to my train of thought and process was exhausting. I got about a tenth of what I wanted to get done finished and then it was time to go.

By now, everyone was home and I wandered through the kitchen to grab my purse. I literally had a complete mom tantrum. It was a cluttered disaster every single direction I looked. I announced that I couldn't be awesome at everything and I hated it, I hated the mess and clutter and I felt like I was drowning under the weight of it all. How could I write a book, run a business from home, be a wife, a mom, and stay on top of this house!! My kids looked sad. I felt both guilty and embarrassed about it. I don't think we need to be stoic or emotionless in front of them but they didn't need to see or hear that from me. They don't need to take that on and my oldest really takes that kind of outburst to heart. I'm not proud of it and I wish it didn't happen. But they actually banded together while we were out and did a whole bunch of work to get the house tidy. I was able to apologize to them for my outburst, to tell them that I loved them and that being their mom is my absolute favourite thing and they are not a burden to me, and to be vulnerable with them. It still feels silly that I let myself get to that point, but at the same time, I will fight to keep the guilt away. As a person of faith, I spent a lot of time praying that God would allow my kids to see how hard I work to support and love them and their dreams, and also how I fought for my own dreams and goals too, while we still showed up for the people in our lives, even when it was hard.

I honestly don't know if the mom guilt train ever stops. Certainly, even through the teen years, it may even ramp up even more. I do not have teens yet so I am not speaking from personal experience but I do know that teens are a whole new world of parenting. People often like to say to parents of small children, "Oh, just wait until they get bigger, this is nothing," which, I happen to feel is a very unhelpful statement in general. When you are in the throes of toddlerhood and you think you are going to lose your ever-loving mind when they come out of bed for the hundredth time with a new complaint or the same recycled one, basically holding their eyelids open because they are so tired but they "can't sleep," and you are trying to get something done or even just go to bed yourself once they are asleep, you are longing for the day when they are teens and they resort to their room and never come out.

As we have talked about before, this is one of the conundrums of parenthood, you often spend much of your time wanting what you do not have. When you are in the throes of being needed and talked to endlessly, you want them to not need you or want to talk to you for even ten minutes. And when they are teens, you long for them to want you and want to talk to you for ten whole minutes. Oh, if we could just bottle it all up and spread it out evenly through all the years, wouldn't that be incredible?

In the teen years, kids are far more independent with more access to more things and opportunities that can have deeper long-term consequences when they make bad choices. Let's be honest, is there is a teen out there that did not make at least a few bad choices over the years? There are always moms attached to those teens. Moms feeling guilty for the choices those teens are making, blaming themselves for being too hands-on, not hands-on enough, not paying enough attention to what may have been happening under their roof, worrying they were smothering their children, or worrying they gave them too much room to do their own thing. Dear moms, you did not fail. Despite what choices your teens are making right now, you did not fail. They are independent thinkers that are pushing boundaries, testing the waters, seeing how far they can go and what they can do. This is part of the teen way.

Some will go so much farther, some will not. Much of this comes down to personality as much as anything else. You could be raising five different children and you already know that what worked for one does not work for the next and on it goes.

Kids have a way of turning out completely different regardless of how they are parented the same. You did not get it all right, none of us does. Forgive yourself, ask your children to forgive you, move on. Let it go because it does not serve either of you to hold on to wrongs. Let us use all our parenting screw ups to teach our children valuable life lessons. One of them being that when we are forgiven, that is in the past. This does not mean that there are not honest conversations about earning trust back when it is broken, consequences for actions and the process of repairing relation-ships. Yet the act of forgiving them, is that you do not dwell on the error and keep using it against them. It means that you now focus on the restoration process. What a gift to give your children to see you navigate the process of restoration with them. This is a life skill that many adults truly lack.

The whole process of parenting is one of constantly questioning when to push away and when to hold them close. Just tonight, my three-year-old had a little dance performance in front of a large group of people. Her very first. I left her with her little class in the hall and went in to get a place to watch. I heard a wail in the hall and wondered if it was her, and then a minute later her dance teacher was crouched down beside her at the door showing her where I was, and saying that I would be there the whole time. My daughter threw up her arms and yelled, "Huggie!!" I reached out and she ran to me. I hugged her quickly and sent her back. She looked back with the most devastated look on her face as she walked away with her arms stretched out for me, but she listened to her teacher. I looked back and five other moms had seen the whole thing and they were clutching their own hearts in sympathy for mine. I felt the comradery in their faces, that they felt my inner turmoil. They understood the torture I felt in my heart. I hated seeing her sad and I wanted to pull her close, but I also knew she was excited and ready for this. The mom right beside me said, "We never know how far to push, hey?" and it is so true. We never really know. My daughter came out and did amazing, and walked out of that place shouting, "*I love ballet!*" She was so proud of herself and I was so proud of her. I knew she could do it. In that moment it is so hard to push past the emotions, to trust that our choices are for their benefit.

One day when I was disciplining my child, I had this realization about why parents have been saying, "This hurts me more than it hurts you," probably since the beginning of time. It really does hurt our hearts on such a deep emotional level. But it matters. True, follow-through discipline hurts both of us, but it also creates children that know how to obey, to have boundaries, listen, be respectful and consider others more than themselves. But it sure hurts to follow through. If I am totally honest, sometimes I am terrible at follow-through. I like to think I am good at it, but some days I am just not. Especially on the days where I know the consequences will impact me too. It could be my time to get something else done, or my time visiting with a friend I have been looking forward to and I find myself silently begging them to just obey for my sake, if nothing else. But if the truth be told, I am my worst version of myself as a mom when I feel like my children do not take me seriously because of my lack of follow-through. I start talking about the lack of respect, I raise my voice, I feel horrible and guilty about the job I am doing as a mother. It spirals into a place that is not edifying to me or my children, and it does not show them a good example at all. Sometimes, I think it is a little gift when in the midst of my own mom tantrum, one of my children will come up to me and say, "I love you mom." My littlest is especially good at this. She will come up to me and say, "Mom??" and I will say, "What??" in the most irritated tone because I am expecting another question about why they have to do something, or another way they can do something *other* than what I asked, and she says, "I just love you." Guilt, gratitude, humility, it all flows over me in that moment.

You will never perfect this mom gig; chances are you will often look at it through the lens of mom guilt. You will have good days and bad days, overwhelming days and too tired days, days where you feel like you nailed it and days where you stand in the kitchen and sob because you are so exhausted you just can*not* go on. But you know what you will do? You will keep going. That's what moms do. You will forget their lunches or pack all the lunches into one backpack and nothing in the other one. You will forget to pick up your kid on the third day of kindergarten at the right time, and when you get there and he will be the only one standing there all alone with the teacher. She will also hand you your credit card because someone found it lying on the ground near the school, and you will slink off with your child, feeling like a failure.

You won't have the right outfit clean on the right day every time. Your kids will call you the worst mom in the world at some point and they will shout, "Just so you know, *I don't feel love!*" at the top of their lungs as they stomp up the stairs. When you go up to talk about whatever the issue is, they will inform you that "You love all the other kids in the house more than me, and you just don't love me." It will tear your heart apart when it happens. Except for the odd time when it is so incredibly ridiculous that you have to fight back a bit of a smirk at the dramatics. Sometimes, you will offer the wrong snacks and your kids will just keep shouting, "No, I just want a snack!!" in the most unreasonable fashion, and you will have absolutely no idea what they want and it will be in a room full of other people, so you desperately try to keep your cool while your small child freaks out and you have no idea how to even fix it.

But then, there is the majority of time when you slay this job. Where you anticipate what outfit they need before they ask and they look at you in awe when you hand it to them, or when you are already on your way into their room with their favourite stuffed animal or blanket before they even knew they needed it. You will get them to all the things at the right time, including figuring out how to get them fed when there is not time to do it all. You will get the hot lunch forms and money in, the agendas signed, the paperwork filled out, the bills paid, the groceries stocked, the schedules meticulously timed out, lunches packed, water bottles ready to go, seasonally appropriate attire for everyone on the way out the door, and you will have a stockpile of clothes, coats, footwear, and other extras in the trunk of the vehicle to be ready for anything. You know who wants crusts on, crusts off, who is having peanut butter and jam, who is having just jam and who wants peanut butter on one side and jam on the other but not touching in the middle.

You have this insane motherboard of details in your brain at all times and more often that not, you nail it. It does not always look pretty, and sometimes you are racing around Costco looking for the stuffed animal that you said no to bringing in but it was a fight so you said yes and now it is lost, just like you said it would be, but you retrace your steps until you find it. You go to the toy store because your kid asked Santa for one specific toy in those little blind bag-type containers and Santa does not get it wrong, so you spend twenty minutes sitting on the floor looking through a tiny hole at the colors you can see and hoping against all hope you choose the right one. On Christmas morning when he opens it and Iron Man tumbles out, you imagine yourself fist pumping the air and yelling, "Nailed it!" but you just quietly revel in the look of sheer delight on their faces that you made the magic happen. This is what we do as moms, we make magic happen out of what is nothing some days. You help them find the wonder in the little things. You keep it all running and it is nothing short of remarkable.

What we do right is so much more than what we do wrong. Where we excel, show up and be excellent as moms is more of the norm. Not to mention, the portion of time where we are just operating in the day-to-day doing the mundane mom tasks with contentment and thankfulness that this is our life and we get to do this. The times where we fail, where we are not our best, this is just a small fraction of the time. Yet, this is where we often choose to camp. I know I do it. I think about all the things I did not do right instead of all the things I did do right. I camp out on the guilt and I struggle to find joy in my day.

Friends, let us stand together and help each other see the ways we are doing things right. Let us recognize where we showed up, where we influenced these little people to be better versions of themselves. Let us choose joy and gratitude rather than guilt. We cannot do this all on our own. It is not the way we are wired. May we recognize each other when we see things that our friends do well. Speaking truth, life, and encouragement over each other. When I was standing there feeling like my heart was breaking as my daughter walked away crying and reaching for me, and I turned and saw five moms holding their hearts and feeling that with me, who told me that it is good to see them fly but it sure hurts when we are in the launching stage, I felt seen. I felt like I was doing something right. We need to see each other and raise each other up. No one else is going understand this more than a band of moms that feel the same emotions to their core.

113

16.

Finding a Purpose in Every Season

There is not a mom out there that would tell you that motherhood is not her purpose. That the act of raising her babies is not her number one priority. This chapter is not trying to negate that purpose or say that is not the most important job that we have in life. It absolutely is. But being a mom is complex, and like every child, is wildly different from the next, so is the level of fulfilment motherhood brings to each different woman. For one mom, this might be the only purpose and dream she has ever had and motherhood fills her with so much joy. Her patience runs deep and there is nowhere else she would rather be. For another mom, her only dream may have been the career she was laser-focused on since she was a girl, and she was heading straight to the top when she got pregnant unexpectedly and, while she adores her child more than life itself, she struggles with where that fits into the only dream she ever had that didn't include children.

Not only are all of our dreams different, but so are the ways our dreams are able to fit into the seasons of life we are in at any given time. Add in the judgment we place on ourselves and the judgment from outside influence on what we should or should not be doing as mothers, and it can feel like you're being tossed around in a sea of uncertainly about what your purpose even is.

If you are the mom that feels like her sole purpose and mission in life is raising children and you are in your element the most when you are home with your kids, raising them, maybe home-schooling them, sitting, reading, doing crafts, and nurturing these little souls, it might seem completely foreign to you that someone else would not find the same joy in those things. Do not for a moment feel like you need to be looking for another purpose. If this is filling your cup, then you just keep giving that gift of your best self to your kids. You keep blessing them with the first fruits of your time, your patience, and your efforts. You will also be such a gift to other moms. You will be such a treasure to them as they watch you nurture your babies and learn little nuggets of mothering from you. You are so deeply invested in this role as a mom that you will have so much valuable advice and information to share with women as they start their journey of motherhood. They will see you, watch you, and seek you out to help them learn how to be the best version of themselves as a mom for their kids. Unapologetically be that gift to your kids and to other moms around you.

For that mom that spent all those years at home with her babies and loving it, it might be later in life as your children grow, they need you less, and then eventually move out of the home that you are feeling lost and lonely. Uncertain. You are dreaming of grand-kids but in this in between season, who are you and do you have purpose and value? Yes! You have so much value. You are a gift. Maybe you can come alongside some young moms that could use your support, someone to help them find their way in those early years when it feels like motherhood is eating us alive some days. We all need amazing mentors. Or maybe you can find something totally different, like nursing homes where you can sit, visit, play games, and bless the sweet residents that are longing for company. A non-profit organization that could use another pair of hands. Along the way as you have raised kids, there have been different things you have experienced with your kids that have given you joy and piqued your interest. Take some time to think about those things, and what you can do that will bring you joy. Remember that you are never too old to start something new. There is never a time in our life with we can't dream bigger, learn new things, and grow a different part of ourselves. Your kids were your heart and soul, being near them was your everything. They still are but they don't need you the same way. The world had to wait for what you have to offer. Now is the time to give the world the gifts that you blessed your kids with for all those years.

For the mom that has a career she loves, and does not want to give that up, don't. And if you have a dream of pursuing a career and you had kids before you went for it, don't let that keep you away from your dream. You might take more time to get there, or you might start later than you planned, but there is so much time in life to pursue what you have always dreamed of. Never tell yourself that it is too late to go for it. When you are in a career you love, you have so much to offer that profession. Whether you are a professional barista or a world-renowned surgeon, the world needs you. People that get their coffee every day need your smile, your warmth, the way you make them feel remembered and seen, the way you learned who they were and what was happening in their life and actually asked the next time they were in. The world needs more light, more love, more kindness; and if you are giving that to people while you make their coffee, thank you for sharing your gifts with the world. If you are literally saving lives and have some of the steadiest hands, the most amazing knowledge, the incredible bravery that it takes to open someone's body and do something to give them a new quality of life that was not there before, the world needs your gifts and talents. It will take work and balance to figure out how to work outside the home and be Mom for your kids. But nothing is impossible. Your kids need to see you giving the world the gifts you were given, doing the things you were called to. They will see you giving of yourself and they will learn from that, and they will see that they can be anything they want to be.

Then there is the mom that may work outside the home to make ends meet, or maybe she stays home with the kids but it is not as soul filling as she wants it to be. Is this you? You are stuck somewhere feeling like you don't know what your passion is? You feel guilty that your kids alone aren't filling your cup? You're longing for more and there are dreams inside of you that you may or may not have stopped actually dreaming about a long time ago, because this just isn't your season to dream bigger. You are maxed out where you are at. Do not stop dreaming! Let yourself start to dream again. Dreaming is so good for the soul and it starts to allow you to see new possibilities that did not exist before. The more you focus on the dreams inside of *you*, the more you still start to see different opportunities and doors that might open to start to allow you to do some things that bring you fulfilment.

Our kids need to see us dream. Every one of us was created for a reason, with gifts and talents to share with our kids, with our spouses, our friends, and the world. Maybe your have to work a job to help make ends meet in order to be able to actually pursue a dream or a calling. The job or career does not have to be the purpose. Maybe you dream about going to another country on a mission-type trip with your family to build houses and help people in Third World countries, or about helping a non-profit organization that ignites a fire inside of you, or about writing a book, taking a wellness class, learning how to cook better, starting a home-based business, or taking up a sport or a hobby that you always wanted to do. It might be that you have to start small. Only an hour or two a week. We all have room to drop a TV show or something to make room to do something that starts to set our hearts on fire.

Sometimes I think back to past seasons in my life and consider how busy I felt in those times. That is not to negate how I felt then or to make people think that I don't think they are busy if they don't have kids. But I think we expand our capacity over time in order to allow ourselves room to do all the things that matter to us. The seasons ebb and flow as well. Babies and toddlers are busy in one way, because they need us to physically do all the things for them and keep them alive. Older kids are more independent but tend to have more activities, homework, social engagements, and life outside of the home that we must navigate. I have never actually met a parent of teenagers yet that did not tell me that the season of toddler busyness didn't begin to compare to the season of busyness with teenagers. I also haven't met a mom of toddlers and babies yet that didn't have a look of daggers in their eyes when they heard those parents of teenagers say that either.

We all have those seasons when it brings tears to our eyes to think about adding in more. It can feel like it would be easier to step away from a career you love for a time, and maybe it is for you. But if that feels like you are settling, I would encourage you to spend more time thinking about how maybe you can rework things to continue to at least pursue your career part-time. If that is your calling, your passion, the world needs you there. It can also feel like you don't have room to pursue something else that matters to you and gets you excited. I think you can. I think there is almost always a way. My husband wanted to join a rotary club so that he could give back to our community in a practical tangible way. He found one that meets before his work day for breakfast, early on Tuesdays. It was the only time we could fit it in without impacting our other responsibilities. If you would have told me that I had time to write a book when I was already busy with our three kids, working my business from home, church, commitments, and trying to keep up with relationships, I would have laughed. We made a way. We made room for each other to each have time. We did a few more nights of solo bed times. We share the load at home. My laundry rarely gets folded. My floors are washed less often. Where I did not think there was room, I prayed that my capacity would be expanded. We dream on our own and we dream together, but we let ourselves dream.

Finding our purpose in every season can be difficult. Each season brings its own challenges. As mothers, our children will always be our first priority. This is good and right. It is necessary and beautiful and we would not choose to have it any other way. Whether that purpose is enough, or it is not, know beyond a shadow of a doubt, that how you are feeling is not wrong. Not needing anything else is amazing. Needing more, a career or some other dream or passion, is also an incredible thing. Because we as women were all created perfectly, with gifts and talents that the world needs. Those dreams were put there for a reason. It is a gift to our children to see us rise up and fight for what sets our hearts on fire. This is where we can be the best version of ourselves for them. This is where we can show them that their dreams matter, that we are going to stand behind them for the rest of their lives, cheering them on, championing *their* dreams, because adults are allowed to go hard after what they love too. The world needs to be filled with moms full of dreams that do not play small, that raise their children to go out into the world and be everything they were created to be.

17.

Mom Fail

Here's the thing. I wrote this whole book about moms being enough. About how we need to talk about this life and share our experiences. We have to band together, love each other and be the champions for each other. That there is never a time when you have failed so completely that you are not enough for your child. I wrote about it. I believe it. I leaned into the calling that it was for me to share this book. Then, in the middle of it, I had one of my very own lowest points ever as a mother.

Talk about wondering if you are enough. Plus, who gave me the right to talk about it and write about it when I am sitting here wondering if I am enough? Fearing that I have left lasting scars that he is going to talk about for the rest of his life? This job is no joke and you can go through a day that is just like every other day and then the wheels start to wobble on the cart. No big deal, you can get this back on the rails. Suddenly the whole thing is careening as fast as it can down a hill, the wheels are off, and you do not even know what to do at this point. Have you ever been there? Sobbing your face off, desperate, unsure, and you are pulling the car over to send a desperate message to the person that you know will pray for you right now, with no details.

This, my friends, is where the trenches feel deep. Mothering hurts. There could be a thousand reasons that you got to this point. It doesn't really matter to be honest. For right now, you are here and it is desperately hard and you are going to have to make some sort of decision. Take some deep breaths. Pray. Trust your gut. Do what comes to your mind in that moment.

Today, my boys came home from school and it was just a regular day. It was the first day back to school after Christmas break and they were probably a little bit tired and still in holiday hangover mode. My younger son had missed out on a hockey game on the weekend because of an attitude issue that we resolved later, and my husband promised he could go to the next one, just the two of them. My older son has a bit of a hockey addiction and he is the one that loves going to the games, reads stats, knows the players, the rules, the details, and he hates to miss the games. He got to go to both games on the weekend and usually goes with his dad and brother. However, in this one case, my husband felt like my younger son needed some time just the two of them. My older son was ready to basically sell his birthright to get his brother to say he could come too. The game was five days away, but he was already working hard on his little brother. It was relentless and getting annoying so I asked him to stop. He would not stop.

I am not entirely sure how it spiraled from there, but I asked them to get ready to go pick up their sister, and my oldest was now in a mood. He started in on how he was a terrible brother that should never have siblings. That he just punches them and cannot help himself, which, for the record, he does not do, generally speaking, unless he and his brother are wrestling or getting a little pushy with each other at times. He does not randomly injure his siblings as a rule. He started to tell me that God made him that way and I should sell him. It seemed funny at the time and I joked for a

121

minute that I would finish what I was doing and put him up for sale. The next thing I realized was that he had gone upstairs. The self-deprecating comments were in full force. I pull him into my lap to snuggle him, which usually helps, but he pulled away, he was goofing off, not listening to my words, and I was starting to get frustrated.

I asked the kids to get into the van because we were running late. My older son got into the back and started in on me. His words were breaking my heart. I started to cry and asked him to stop talking and said we could talk at home. On it went. I stopped the car to text my friend to pray right now. I called my husband and told him I was bringing our child to his office. Feeling so broken and that I had responded so poorly to him, I was at a loss. I'm his mom. I am supposed to be able to fix things. Work it out. Hold him. Love him. I suddenly felt like I could not fix this and I needed to step away from him. Once he knew I was dropping him off with his dad he sat quietly, also crying in the back. I have never felt so sad and like the biggest failure as a mom.

Tears stream down my face as I type this. I felt so desperate and low as a mother. For every one of us, these moments are hopefully few and far between, and maybe some of you have never been there or won't ever be there, but they happen. Sometimes the cir-cumstances seem very benign and unlike other day-to-day stuff, and it can feel almost surreal that it actually got to this point, as in this case. Other times there are significant circumstances leading up to it. The situations play out longer and the stakes are even higher. Regardless of how or why you ended up there, it feels dark and lonely. The darkest moments where we have to fight our way out of it. Where we have to choose to step away from our child, even for a short period of time for both of our sakes. This is not a failure. This is necessary. This is where we show our children that when there are times in conflict where we can not find a solution, rather than saying words that might actually hurt for a lifetime, we can step away. Maybe we get outside counsel. Maybe we just take time to breath and think. These are appropriate ways to manage a conflict. In some of my lowest moments at a mom, there is room to show my kids humility and grace. I am grateful that there is never anything that happens for no reason. If we are looking for the teaching moments and we are willing to accept that we often have to humble ourselves to our kids, we can show them so much more than we maybe ever dreamed we could in those low points. Give yourself space in the midst of this and know that it is okay to step away, if your can leave your child in a safe place.

An hour later my husband brought our son home. They had sat and talked about the lies my son was telling himself, and how they were not serving him. They prayed together. He said my son was a different child as soon as they finished. He walked into my arms when he got home and said, "I'm sorry, Mommy." We snuggled together and talked about how we felt, and we said, "I love you." Forgiveness. Restoration.

Motherhood is messy, painful, and hard. We were still chosen by God to be moms to the children in our families. We were hand-picked and exactly what they need. It will not always be pretty but we can always look for the good, for the lessons, for the beauty and restoration on the other side. Give yourself space to care for your heart when this happens. When you have an emotional hangover, do not rush it away or push it away. Give yourself the space to feel it. Lean into it and learn from it. Digest it. Take away what is good and what you can learn, and then let go of the rest and allow it to wash away.

18.

You Are Enough

As I have written this book, I have laughed and cried all by myself in front of my computer. I have sought out words to bless those of you reading this book, and I have cried tears over all the things that it encompasses. Tears over how hard mom life is. Tears over the exploding love we feel for these little people that we have been blessed with. Tears over the constant push and pull of emotions that takes us from one end of the spectrum to the other and back, sometimes in the span of minutes!

The reality of motherhood is that there is nothing harder. But you don't know that before you get there, because you cannot fathom the emotions that come with raising your own children. Regardless of which stage you are in, do not think for a second that it shouldn't be this hard. There is not a single stage, season or age that comes with a manual to make it easy. Loving someone as fiercely as you love your child, but accepting their own free will and choice to make decisions that you will not always agree with, whether it is drawing on your new couch with a Sharpie at three years old or doing drugs as a teenager, makes it *impossible* for this to be easy. For those of you missing those days with toddlers and you want to tell those new moms that are in the thick of it that

"One day, you will miss this," don't say that. Instead, say, "I miss that stage, can I come and hold your baby while you have a nap?" or "I miss my toddlers, can I come and do crafts and play with yours while you run some errands alone?" For the moms in the thick of the toddler stage that sees their friend with teenagers who is struggling, go for coffee with her and give her a safe place to share her heart. She might just be needing a judgment-free zone, and you will probably go home a little more thankful for your toddlers.

Regardless of how you are feeling today, do you love your child unconditionally? I would imagine the answer is yes. Do you get up in the middle of the night when you hear their cries, despite the fact that your body is screaming no, I'm sure you do. Are you feeding them, clothing them, loving them, hugging them, kissing them and showing up for them even when you feel like you have nothing left? Yes. Of course you are! I didn't ask if you are execut-ing this perfectly and whether their hair is combed and they ate six servings of vegetables today, I asked if you met their basic needs. Moms of teens, are you taking an interest in their interests and making them feel seen? I bet you are at least trying! Whether you barely scraped together the basic needs of your small children, or you managed healthy meals with great snacks, you baked together, you read three stories, laughed and cuddled together and made a craft and you feel like supermom today, *you were enough*. Whether your teen sat down and had a thirty-minute conversation with you or just gave you a grunt on the way by, *you were enough*. Both of those moms showed up with all the love in the world for their kids. Both of those moms gave every little bit of the capacity they had that day, and that is remarkable.

As our kids grow, their needs change but the fact that they need us does not. Depending on the child and the age, they may not express it, realize it or think it, but at the end of the day, they need their mom. I find as my oldest grows, how I parent him changes and evolves. He is only seven and he is my first "bigger kid." Some days it feels like pure magic to watch him be an amazing oldest sibling. To be generous and kind to his brother and sister. My heart swells to see his heart serve and love them. I have to remind myself at other times, that this is part of his true character when we have not seen it for awhile and he is struggling to be his best self. This is a very tricky time, because they are caught between big and little. They are still a little bit interested in the things that are for littler kids but then have this desire to be like the bigger kids. They have a hard time knowing the boundaries and limits to their questions, jokes, sense of humour (that often does not seem that funny to anyone else) and their pestering "I'm just being funny" behaviour.

So how do we love them and build them up without squashing their little spirits? It can be hard to see them for all their gifts when much of their behaviour is just plain annoying at times. I do love it when we have those remarkable days where I see every little bit of the things that I love about him shining through. I try to praise him extensively on those days. Recently, we have come out of a bit of a rough patch where it felt like it was hard to like much about his behaviour. It felt entitled and annoying, and at one point he was basically shouting at me every time I said anything to him. It took everything in me to maintain a calm voice because my inside self was not calm at all. I finally asked him to please go lie in his bed. It had become clear that he was completely irrational and this was not going anywhere in the right direction. He went to the stairs. I asked him to go to his bed. He said no. I said yes. This battle of wills continued until he was in his bed, with his head under the covers yelling, "You just love the other two more than me!" Only by the grace of God in this instance did I keep a level head. But my inner mother voice told me that he needed his love tank filled more than he needed a lecture and consequences.

There is not a magic formula for all of this stuff. When do they need a firm discussion and consequences, when do they need a gentler approach, when do they need a blend of both? There are not cut and dried answers to this. Give yourself grace as you navigate each situation. What seems like a bad habit you are noticing that you need to nip in the bud, and what seems like an over the top reaction that is out of character? Trust your mom instincts; they will not likely lead you astray. You may have a hard time holding your cool—we all do. It felt miraculous when I was able to just stay calm and not yell. If you pray, pray that God would give you patience. If you have another tool that allows you a quick outlet to regain your composure like counting to five or taking some deep breaths, I highly recommend doing it in this moment. When you are both ready, have a good conversation.

The beauty of kids as they get older, even six and seven, is that you can start having true conversation. It might be simple but do not underestimate the power of letting them be heard and have the opportunity to speak freely to you. Recently, as my kids grow and change, I often hear, "I don't even know why I am crying." We have all had those days, haven't we? Over our lifetimes we have had moments where we feel big feelings and we don't even know why or how to express them to someone else. On this particular day when I was ready, I put on a show for my other two and asked them to give us space, and went up to my older son's room. I climbed up his bunkbed ladder, dug him out of his blankets, and pulled him close. His tears made my shirt wet and I held him for what felt like a long time until I felt his little body relax against mine. When I asked him what was wrong today, he said he didn't know. We talked for a while and I came to the conclusion that my son, with a love language of physical touch, who is growing bigger, becoming more independent and doesn't crawl into my lap for snuggles as often, needed to be held. I was so grateful that my instinct told me to just be with him. After a period of time, and some conversation about attitudes and that it still is not acceptable to yell at people and make these weird growling faces and start hissing (kids express themselves in the funniest ways sometimes), that I love him and I would like to just have a re-do on the last hour or two of our day. It was a day that I felt like I got it right.

Isn't it amazing when we have those days? Where we feel like our motherhood game is strong? But what about the days that we don't? When our game feels weak. Where our own fuses are short, we are carrying much of our own stress through the days or maybe you haven't been getting good sleep at night because of sick kids, or other sleep interruptions. Instead of feeling like you got it right, you feel like you yelled, responded in anger, and flared up the situation. There will be another opportunity for a re-do. Learn from this opportunity; plan ahead with some tools to maintain your cool next time so you are ready. Some days we feel like we nailed it. Some days we don't. Some days we realize after the fact that something we thought was a failure, actually wasn't. Sometimes we handle something a certain way and it doesn't feel good inside of us. These are the intricacies of navigating motherhood. The key is that each and every moment and situation, we showed up for it. The good, the bad, and the ugly—and that is what matters.

Every mom I have met that is in the tween years bears this look that is somewhere between perplexed, confused, and scared. This is where we are trying our absolute best to set our kids up for the big world that is coming, while maintaining this sense of innocence that might still be there. There is so much about this season of life that is complex. I know personally I never look back and think,

"I wish I was twelve or thirteen again, or even fifteen or sixteen." I do not miss that season in life. I think everyone has different memories of that time in their life, but with the peer pressure, the changing that goes in inside our bodies during these years, the expectations and major life changes that are coming over the next few years, this is an intense season and we as moms are both an anchor and a target. They need us to be their security and safety net. They need us to stand firm, but we are also going to take a beating in this season. Our hearts are going to be broken over and over by words said, actions taken, as well as things left unsaid and actions not taken.

I have some pretty amazing mom friends that are there, some are on their way into those years and some that have survived them. So, I keep relying on their knowledge and expertise here, but honestly, from what I can see, these are the years where you can feel the hardest on yourself as a mom, and yet, it probably gets talked about the least. It seems like there is more conversation about how you aren't failing as a mom when your kids are small, but there is a lot more personal judgment on ourselves as we watch our kids make bad choices and a lot of external judgment that their bad choices reflect badly on the parents and how they raised them as teens. What I imagine, is that there are a lot of parents that suffer in this silent place of fear and judgment as their teens do what every teen on earth does: make some really dumb choices. But, as I said earlier, behind every teen is a mom that sheds tears in her room at night because she taught him better, or she raised her differently than that, and they are embarrassed, angry, hurt, frustrated, or a combination of all of these things while they watch their kids do the opposite of what they know is right.

Moms, read this part one thousand times if you have to. You are not responsible for the poor decisions your teens make. You did not fail. I see you thinking back over every thing you have ever taught them, and taking inventory of where you could have possibly gone wrong. As I write this, I cry tears for your hearts. You did not go wrong. You are not wrong. You are not a failure. You are a mom that loves that bone-headed teenager more than anyone else on this entire planet, hoping they do better, praying for their safety, and loving them in spite of their bad decisions and choices. This is your job. To stand in the gap and pray for them. To be the safe place to land when they come back. It does not mean you have to be pushed over, that you don't hand out consequences and have firm conversations about their choices. This is also part of your job.

But you also make sure they know, even if they do not express their understanding in any way (remember all those times your toddlers and small children heard you but acted like they didn't and it drove you crazy, it was preparing you for the teen years), that they are loved. Nothing is going to change that. This is what moms do best. You may weep, punch things and swear and break stuff in the privacy of your own room; this season does not come without its fair share of hard emotions. But if you didn't love them so deeply, none of this would hurt so much.

The moms that helped me understand this season also gave me so much hope for these years too. These can be some of the best times of raising kids too. Where you get to connect on a different level. Where real, deep conversations happen with them. When you do get to hang out with them, it is fun. They are so funny and you start to see who they are going to be as adults. As the technology world comes faster and more furious all the time, this time together can be harder to carve out and that real connection can be harder. Fight for it. Fight for the times of connecting. If you can, sit down and have at least some meals together during the week. Maybe you have a technology-free zone when you are driving to activities. However that looks for you and your family, carve out some time to talk to each other. Maybe the moments of joy are few and far between for your teens, or maybe you have the gift of having them around more often than others do, either way, savor the moments. You can raise two kids exactly the same way and one will fight to not connect and the other will fight to connect with you. Don't hesitate to take interest in their interests. Even if it is weird and you do not understand any of it and it makes you feel so old.

Remember when you were dating your significant other and you did things that maybe you never would have imagined doing or you took interest in something that you thought was so boring? It did not make any sense, but you wanted them to know that they mattered to you and that you cared about the things that mattered to them. Do this for your kids, too. The more they see you accepting them for who they are, the more they will actually want to connect with you.

You can make it through the teen years. Your oldest might seem like a breeze and your second one blows your mind. Maybe your oldest gave you an entire head of grey hairs and you were bracing for another storm, and the next one makes this whole thing seem like a walk in the park. We are all on different paths. Care for each other. Do not hesitate to reach out to your friends with teens and make sure they are doing okay. What if we opened up the communication about how hard it can be to raise teens? Maybe you have an experience that will give another mom hope. What if we also shed light on what can be great about it? If instead of saying to a mom of littles, "Oh, you just wait for the teen years" in a voice laced with sarcasm, we said, "This season is hard. But savour what is good because the next one will have its own challenges that are different. It will have moments to savour, too. It looks like you are doing your very best here right now. Hang in there." What a much more helpful and beautiful response. Acknowledgment of the hard, a reminder to also look for what is good, to savour what you can, and a word of encouragement in the middle of a rough patch.

It does not matter what season of motherhood you are in. Every one of them has parts that are sucking you completely dry where you feel desperate, unsure of how to proceed and certain that your failure meter is off the charts. There are also parts that you absolutely live for. Moments that make you feel like your heart could explode, your proud mom meter is off the charts and you feel like you are winning at mom life. This is motherhood. It is the best and hardest thing that we will ever do. You will not get it all right, but you will not get it wrong nearly as much as you think you do. I see you showing up every day, and it is incredibly strong and resilient. Well done, friends. Well done.

This summer, as my husband and I were driving down from a day at the lake with family, we got into this whole discussion about a wide variety of things that we had on our plates and the ways that we had filled our summer schedule. There were lots of projects that did not get done around our house that we had planned to get done. However, we showed up in a lot of other places this summer. You see, we love to help people. If we all just showed up a little more when we have the capacity, imagine how much better off we would all be. There are seasons where we have no capacity for more, and there are others that we can rearrange things in order to show up for other people. As we were talking about this, I got all teary and I said to him, more than anything, I want our kids to see that we are people that show up for others. I want them to show up for others because they saw our example. This has become my motto for life. Be someone who shows up.

As I have used that motto over the months since and I thought about it more, it made me think a lot about motherhood and how it is all about showing up. Day in and day out, in the mundane and in the amazing. We show up. For our kids. For our partners. For the teachers that sent a notice home and need supplies or baking or help in the class. For the teams when they need fundraising. For the Sunday school teachers when they need the kids at the Christmas concert practices on time. For your extended family when they need you. For your friend when she had a baby and she needs a meal, or a baby holder. For that person that just lost a loved one and you want to bring them a meal, or some flowers and a hug. For all the things, we show up.

Sometimes showing up is way harder than other times. Even tonight, I had to run out and pick up my daughter. My two sons were pushing each other's buttons in the back of the van. We had to swing by my parents' place for a minute to pick something up and get home in time to make dinner, which was not going to be pizza, nachos or pancakes, so it would definitely get push back from the kids. Our ten-minute stop turned into a forty-minute adventure of the kids not listening and doing the opposite of what I said. I was trying not to yell. Now we were pretty late to get home and make supper. I started prepping the chicken in the instant pot and one child starting yelling, "What is that disgusting smell?" from the living room, and announcing that she was not eating that! I got it all in the instant pot which started cooking, only to give the warning "burnt food" on the front. My husband arrived home from work while I was chatting with the neighbor at the door for a few minutes while holding back our five-month-old labradoodle that wanted to jump, lick, and run away. After she left, my husband showed me a trick to get the dog to just sit (which was done in love and was helpful information), and I basically burst into tears, told him that was great advice when you are the person that everyone in this house listens to, but I am not that person.

"No one obeys, I don't have time to train the dog while I am trying to cook supper and be a nice neighbour, have a quick visit at the door, and my parents must think I'm a terrible mother, and look, I cannot even operate the instant pot without burning dinner and it looks like it might as well just be left over pizza tonight!" Then I turned into his arms and cried.

After that, I wiped my face, finished dinner in a pan on the stove, served it up, which one child went into a complete meltdown over and refused to eat, and told me he would only eat Grandma's food, and ended up going to bed without dinner. Then I managed to get all my children to bed, cuddled, kissed, and assured of my love. Maybe they will remember how much they hated dinner tonight, but I hope, and believe, that they will remember that they were loved.

Showing up does not mean it is a breeze. Showing up does not mean we do not have these moments in the kitchen where we cry about how much we feel like we are failing. Showing up means we keep pressing on in spite of these things. It means we still feed them a healthy meal rather than their three choices every single night that are not the healthiest because it is the path of least resistance. We do take that path from time to time too, when life needs us to. Sometimes we just pick them up and strip them down, find their favourite pajamas, use whatever tools we use to settle them for the night, and hold them tight even when we feel hurt by their words and their actions. Do not let those thoughts and feelings live there. They are not welcome and they will not serve you. Let them go, have a cry. Remind yourself at the end of it all what you did right, and all the ways we are *not* a failure as a mother. Then dust yourself off and keep showing up.

I had a situation come up recently that speaks powerfully to the amazing way that moms come through for other moms. I have one child that really knows how to nail the obscure Christmas request every year. He has a particular brand of stuffed animal that he loves, especially the keychain version of each one. One, in particular, was high on his list and we found it back in the spring. Only to lose it very shortly afterward! I'm sure is it the only one we have ever actually lost. I have scoured every display for months looking for a replacement. He asked me for one again the other night and I said I was sorry but I couldn't find it anywhere. He got this sweet smile on his face and informed me that he would ask Santa! I could feel my heart sink. It was thirteen days until Christmas, I could not find the keychain, even exorbitantly priced online, to arrive before Christmas. So, I did the only thing I could: I put out a post on my social media begging for anyone that had collections of these same stuffed animals that their child had out-grown, to look and see if they could spare me this particular dog, on a keychain. It felt like such a long shot, but it was all I had.

Wouldn't you know, in the span of about fifteen hours, I had dozens of messages from friends, friends I hadn't talked to in years, acquaintances, and even total strangers sending me links online, giving me ideas of where I could look locally, and telling me that they were calling stores in their own cities to ask if they had them, and were going to pick one up for me. Moms (and a couple of men and friends that are not moms), seeing my desperate post, and knowing what it is like to have that kind of pressure to come through for your kids, wanting to help. People that I did not even know, investing time in this, especially at a time of year when time is at a premium. People going out of their way to go to stores in their towns. Talk about showing up for another mom! This is what we do. Those ladies came through for me in such a huge way.

All day the next day I felt the tears of gratitude fill my eyes as I thought about this. How humbling it was to be on the receiving end of simple care and concern, but so much time and love too. Over a small black puppy on a keychain named Tracey that needed to be in that stocking on Christmas day. I love how capable we are to give of ourselves when the opportunity arises.

There is so much about motherhood that is just plain hard. It can be messy, chaotic, and painful. Your heart is always tugged in many directions. The constant fight to rush it by and to stop time and savour every minute. The pendulum of "worth it" and "not worth it" is constantly swinging back and forth. On those tough days, do we go out while we are a hot mess and have a distraction, or do we stay in and not subject the world to all that we are as a collective grumpy group? Do we take a trip when it's more work and time to get ready than the entire trip might be and you have no idea if it is going to be one big disaster, or a sweet little vacation full of amazing memories, a breath of fresh air, and change that your soul needs? Do you cook, clean, or take a nap if you have ten minutes to yourself?

At every turn there is a decision. A yes. A no. Some will turn out beautifully, some will be epic failures. We laugh and we cry our eyes out. There will be days where you think about taking a shower and literally cannot remember the last time you did. Just when you think your kids are at good stages where you really like all of them and find it a little easier to parent them, at least one, if not all, will fall off the wagon into a new stage and you find yourself looking sideways at them the first few times they test you and think, "Huh, you must need to go to bed early," or "Maybe it's the time change or full moon throwing you off," and on it goes for about a week or two until you realize with some disappointment that here you are. A new stage of changing, growing, testing, and more testing. You steel yourself for it. If this is your first, it might take longer to recognize the pattern. If it is your second, third, fifth, or seventh, you give yourself a little pep talk and remind yourself that you are a rock star and you will make it through.

Kids have a funny way of being totally different, just so we don't get comfortable in our parenting styles. You'll meet other moms along the way that, if you are willing to actually be honest and vulnerable when they ask how you are doing, may just validate that they went through that stage too at the same age, and they will bless your heart and encourage you to keep going. Stay strong, Momma. You got this. So much of parenting and motherhood is different from child to child, and yet comfortingly similar. Be open with other moms. Be vulnerable and brave to share your stories. It is in this that we find that comradery, that comfort, the strength to press on in the journey, the light on the other side.

Let us be these women of comradery. Let us be women that do not judge, but rather we ask questions to learn, to hear, to know each other. May we be truly vulnerable with each other so that we can bravely walk beside each other, and lift each other up. In my job as an emergency room nurse, I had many friends that offered support in some of those hard times where I was carrying heavy burdens and I appreciated them, but it was my co-workers, the ones at the bedside with me that truly understood what was happening inside of me. Motherhood is much like this. Until you have been there, you do not fully understand.

I was a friend, not a mom, for many years. I have said to my friends more than once since I had kids, I'm sorry if I was just not a great friend and did not meet your needs when I did not have kids. I just didn't know how it was. So, let us band together as women that do know. It can be hard to expand your capacity when you feel like you are barely keeping your head above water, but there is something beautiful and life-giving about coming together, being brave, having honest conversations, crying together about how this job is hard. Maybe the same mom that you fed before will do the same for you in return when you are having a rough day. This is how we survive the hard days; this is how we can normalize the fact that none of it is Instagram-perfect, those people with clean houses just pushed the mess out of the frame of the picture for a minute. No one is going to make all the same decisions as you are. They don't have the same kids as you. Motherhood needs to be a safe zone of acceptance and understanding. Reassuring another woman that "It's okay, it will be my turn tomorrow or next week. We have all been there and I think you are remarkable." Be the gift of love, encouragement and acceptance to other mom friends, and I guarantee you will also be equally as blessed, if not more.

The other side of motherhood, the magical piece that we cannot put our finger on, the miraculous, unconditional love that wells up from a place inside us that we cannot explain, *that* is the ticket to all of this. This journey is an absolute gift. The fierce love that is like nothing else you have ever known or will ever know again. The fact that we get to do this. We have been blessed beyond measure with one, two, maybe seven children that are ours to love, raise, nurture, value, and hold. From the first moment you hear that little cry and they are placed into your arms, the single biggest and best high on earth, and you know in that moment you are forever changed. You thought you were while you felt this little person grow inside you, but when they arrived earthside and into your arms, that is the true magic and you know nothing is ever going to be the same. There is no going back and no way you would ever choose to. You might think and dream about it from time to time, but the reality is, you wouldn't choose that in a million years because the richness of motherhood is like nothing else. Where you see the strength that you possess that you didn't know was possible, the love you have to give is exponential and unending, and you make sacrifices you never imagined for these little people and learn the true meaning of selflessness.

It is an incredible gift to be the single most important human being to your children. While our love for them is in unconditional, so is theirs for us. While that can be exhausting at times, there is nothing that makes me feel more incredible and empowered than when my children come to me and crawl into my lap and need me. When they sit and hold my cheeks and stare into my eyes and say things like, "You're pretty, Momma."

I can be in the stall in a public bathroom and my daughter is in the next one and I hear this little voice call me, "Mom??"

And I say, "Yes, I'm right here."

And she says, "I love you, Mom."

All day, every day, my daughter tells me she loves me. I'm her person. Her brothers still want me to crawl into their beds and snuggle them at night. These days won't last forever and at the end of the day, it is often a challenge not to rush through those moments, but when I'm on my game, I remind myself to take a deep breath. Savour. Linger. A few extra minutes. A few more back scratches.

We also get to know them better than anyone. We know how they want their sandwich, what flavours they like, what cup is their favourite, or if they want their marshmallows in the hot chocolate or beside it so they aren't soggy. What makes them tick and how to diffuse many situations before they totally derail. We know their warning signs, and when to push harder or hold them closer and stop pushing. We get to know what they love and how simple little things can delight them. Little surprises that we can bring home, and see their faces light up and the breathless sound of their voice as they say, "Thank you Momma, I love it."

The magic and wonder of Christmas is one of my favourite times of year. It can be busy and full, but the opportunity to create magic for them is all I ever need. I could go through Christmas without a single gift for myself, because I have the privilege of being Santa for these kids. Creating this space of awe and wonder. Hearing their shrieks of delight as they spy the things they asked for, and then try and figure out all the details of how Santa managed to pull all of this off. The twinkle in their eyes, the joy. Where we get to soak it all in and feel like kids again because we experience the magic and wonder through their eyes. This is our gift.

Our children are a gift. Motherhood is a gift. It is hard, beautiful, chaotic, messy, joyful, painful, full of tears, and full of laughter. There are days that you will feel like you were amazing and days where you feel like an utter failure. There will be days when you want to throw in the towel, but a well-timed "Mommy, I love you. You are the best," quickly followed by a deep belly laugh as you lean in and tickle that little person and give them a hundred smooches into the crook of their neck because you actually can't speak yet to say I love you back, because the lump in your throat is too big and you do not want that sweet child to think their words made you sad: The reality is that those were the most magical, perfect words ever spoken. Words that just filled your tank, gave you the strength to go on for another day, to try again tomorrow and to be better next time. Words full of nothing but grace and love because that child sees you as the most amazing person on earth.

If only we could see ourselves through the eyes of our children. If only we could love ourselves as deeply as we love them and they love us. This sweet, sweet grace in the midst of all the chaos that allows us to see the absolute treasure that motherhood is and that you must be doing a lot of things right, because that little person is full of love and that only comes from being loved. Being loved so deeply and unconditionally. Loved by a momma that will never stop being their champion, their biggest fan and their strongest supporter. Sweet moms, *you are enough*. You are *more* than enough. You are strong and courageous. You are brave. You are wildly loved.